What Every Woman Should Know
Lifestyle Lessons from the 1930s

What Every Woman Should Know
Lifestyle Lessons from the 1930s

Pictures and Facsimile Pages from the
Daily Mail

Christopher and Kirsty Hudson

Edited by Sarah Rickayzen

Trans Atlantic Press

Contents

Introduction   7

Cookery   8

Household Hints   28

Fashion   44

Beauty   76

Lifestyle   96

Answers to Correspondents   114

First published in 2008
This edition published by Transatlantic Press in 2010

Transatlantic Press
38 Copthorne Road
Croxley Green, Hertfordshire, WD3 4AQ

© Associated Newspapers Ltd

A catalogue record for this book is available from the British Library.

ISBN 978-0-9558298-1-9/978-0-907176-62-3

Printed and bound in China

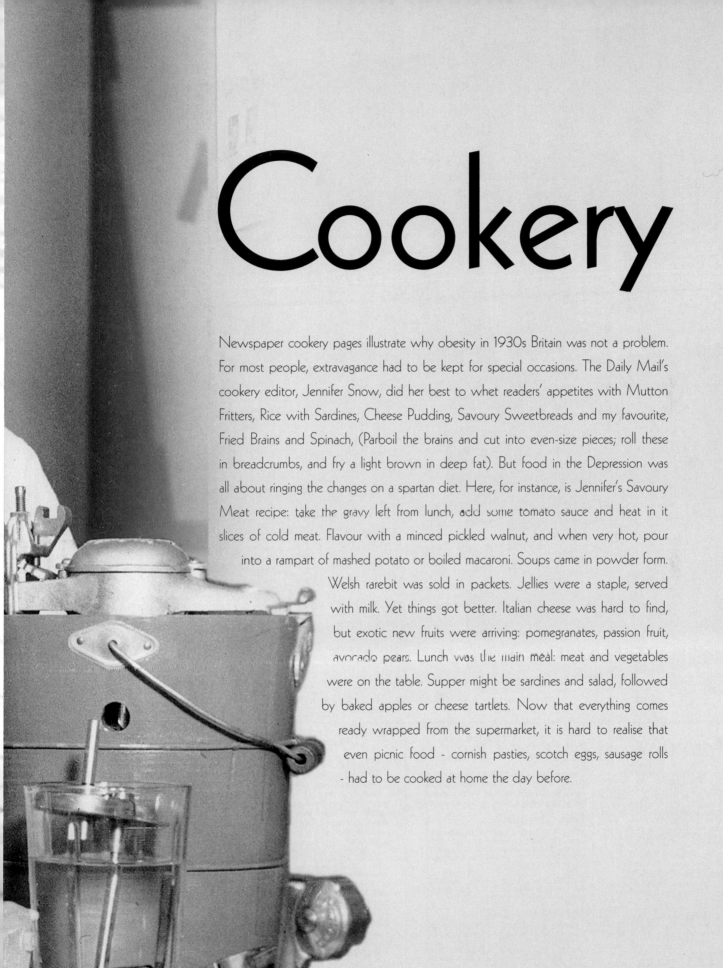

Cookery

Newspaper cookery pages illustrate why obesity in 1930s Britain was not a problem. For most people, extravagance had to be kept for special occasions. The Daily Mail's cookery editor, Jennifer Snow, did her best to whet readers' appetites with Mutton Fritters, Rice with Sardines, Cheese Pudding, Savoury Sweetbreads and my favourite, Fried Brains and Spinach, (Parboil the brains and cut into even-size pieces; roll these in breadcrumbs, and fry a light brown in deep fat). But food in the Depression was all about ringing the changes on a spartan diet. Here, for instance, is Jennifer's Savoury Meat recipe: take the gravy left from lunch, add some tomato sauce and heat in it slices of cold meat. Flavour with a minced pickled walnut, and when very hot, pour into a rampart of mashed potato or boiled macaroni. Soups came in powder form. Welsh rarebit was sold in packets. Jellies were a staple, served with milk. Yet things got better. Italian cheese was hard to find, but exotic new fruits were arriving: pomegranates, passion fruit, avocado pears. Lunch was the main meal: meat and vegetables were on the table. Supper might be sardines and salad, followed by baked apples or cheese tartlets. Now that everything comes ready wrapped from the supermarket, it is hard to realise that even picnic food - cornish pasties, scotch eggs, sausage rolls - had to be cooked at home the day before.

in the Christmas Kitchen

helpful hints from a cook with a camera . . .

ICING THE CAKE YOURSELF?

Then here is the way to set about it. Just let the icing run over the top as you see in the first picture above : it will smooth itself out, and a palette knife dipped in hot water will give the final touch. The sparkling white of royal icing comes chiefly through lengthy stirring, though lemon juice will help further.

And here are some hints about the almond icing. Firm kneading and yet more kneading gives the smooth professional touch to this. It should all be done with the knuckles. Cut a round for the top and a strip for the sides of the cake—it fits better that way—and brushing white of egg over the cake makes the paste stick. A teaspoonful of orange water or rose water to each pound and a half of sugar adds an intriguing flavour.

MINCE PIES

These pies are already figuring in many menus. Brush them with water before dredging them with caster sugar—see picture above—and put them into a fairly hot oven. A brushing with white of egg will make them glossy, but the yolk will give both brown and gloss. Choose which you like—but do let your pastry taste as nice as the filling ! Getting the paste well aerated in the making is more than half the secret of this.

Roast turkey must have its chestnut stuffing, even if the nuts *are* a trouble to prepare. Remove the tops, as shown in the third picture, and bake them for twenty minutes before you can get off the outer and inner skin. Any sieved chestnuts over will make a sauce—a flavouring of lemon and cayenne, please—in case you serve the turkey rechauffé.

THOSE PUDDING BASINS

Basins for Christmas pudding must be really well buttered before they are filled. Have ready a well-buttered round of greaseproof paper for the top. Pudding cloths can now be bought with a tape running round the edge for tying, and a strip of cloth for lifting out of the pot. If you are boiling the puddings and not steaming them, keep the water away from the top. Let the mixture stand for twelve hours before cooking.

BE CAREFUL!

Each ingredient is important for successful Christmas puddings. Flour must be thoroughly dry—warm it if you are not sure——a n d *sieved* in for lightness, as shown in the photograph above. Weigh or measure *everything*, and put the dry ingredients on pieces of greaseproof paper. Break your eggs separately into a cup before adding to a mixture.

> Cut out this page and keep it for reference! It will be tremendously useful during this month's cooking activities.

ON the AUGUST MENU — TRY THESE RECIPES — *By Pearl Adam*

WHEN a month contains a "Glorious Twelfth" it would never do to talk of its food without mentioning grouse.

But most of us will not get beyond mentioning it for the first few weeks of its sojourn at the poulterer's; and even if we did we should not feel inclined to interfere with the majesty of its presence on our tables other than by roasting it first and then grilling it.

Let it merely be remembered by the lucky housewives who do have grouse on the menu that it needs longer hanging than any other game to ensure tenderness, even without a suspicion of highness; that when underdone it is very unpleasant, and that it responds particularly well to being very quickly browned in fat or in a very hot oven and then cooked in greaseproof paper with a nut of butter and a spoonful of water.

Balkan Cold Meat

Sharpen your knives, for this must be cut thinner than the best-cut ham. It is a fine summer dish. Dispose the meat on ice-cold plates, and garnish each with at least six kinds of pickle or chopped salad, with due regard to colour. On the most thunderous evening, meat served like this can be eaten by people who could have sworn it was impossible to swallow anything.

Tomato Dumpling

Cut large, firm tomatoes in two. Scoop out the centre, mix the pulp with very thick cheese sauce, fill the halves with it, tie them together with white cotton, and egg and breadcrumb them twice over. Put them in a covered self-basting dish, with a spoonful of butter, unless you have a deep pan of boiling oil available—and cook for twenty minutes in a moderate oven.

Cheese Marrow Fritters

These are a delicious luncheon dish, especially in hot weather. Slice the marrow and leave it to drain in a colander under a sprinkling of salt for an hour. Then dip it in pancake batter flavoured with grated cheese, and fry it in very hot fat. Sprinkle the fritters with cheese and brown them under the flame.

Pineapple Fruit Cream

This is an excellent way of using up those left-overs of fruit which complicate the day after a tennis party or dinner. There are a few raspberries, or a few strawberries and cherries, and three or four plums, perhaps.

Drain some tinned slices or chunks of pineapple, and tease them out with a fork into their smallest flakes. Put the whole strawberries or raspberries and the stoned cherries or plums with these, and pour over them a cream or beaten-egg sauce. Chill it without icing it, and it will not taste at all like a left-over.

The pineapple syrup will do excellently for a fruit salad next day, or will greatly brighten stewed apples, if used instead of water. If fresh pineapple is available serve the mixture in the scooped-out fruit, with its tuft of leaves as a lid.

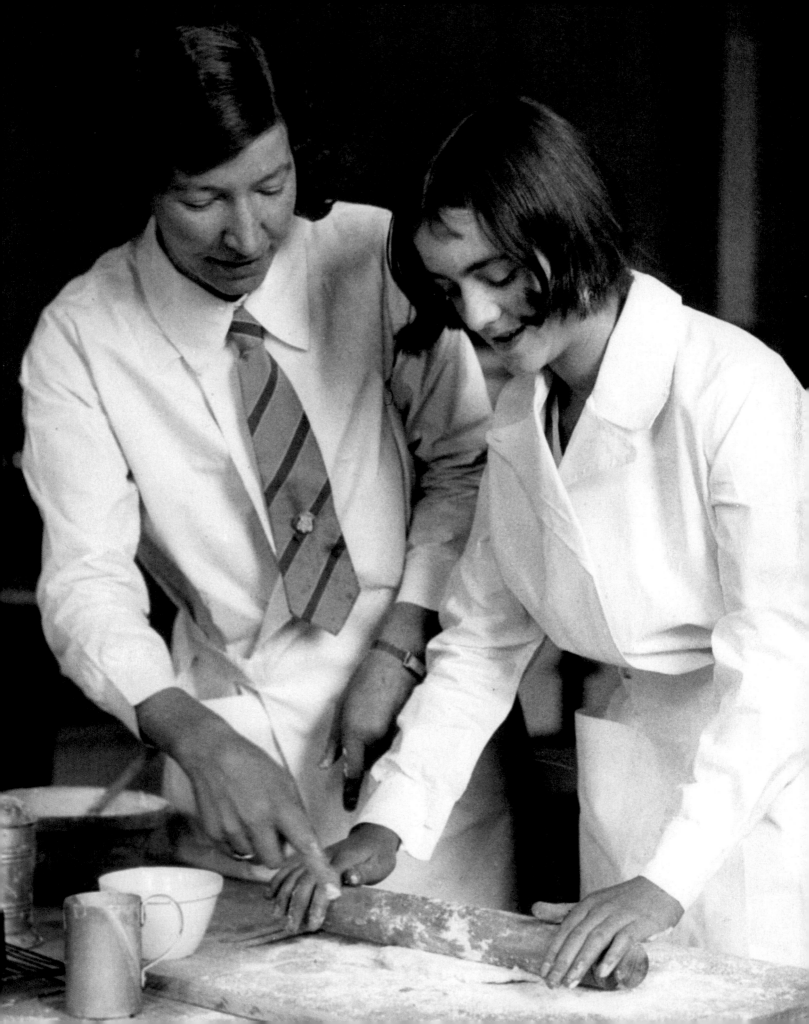

HINTS FOR AMATEUR COOKS

by DORIS B. SHERIDAN

SECRETS of SUCCESS

"COMMON sense and a good cookery book. That's all you need," said the bridegroom-to-be to Sheila, his fiancée, a typical modern girl with a B.A. degree and a responsible office job.

"That's all very well," put in the fourth member of the party—mathematics mistress at a well-known girls' school, who has taught herself her cookery in the bachelor-woman's flat which is her greatest pride.

"Admitted you need the common sense and the cookery book, but what about the simple things that the cookery books take for granted?"

Practical Tips From Experience

She produced from her handbag a small cookery book—a little gift for Sheila—and, turning its pages, she continued: "Here is a simple example of what I mean.

"In this recipe for macaroni soup half an ounce of macaroni is required, and you are told to add it boiled and rinsed and cut into small rings.

"How can one expect a novice like Sheila to know that macaroni and its fellows spaghetti and vermicelli must go into boiling salted water for anything up to twenty minutes?"

She continued her criticisms through the various sections of the book and we talked cookery for the rest of the evening.

WHEN making a layer cake trim the edges with a very sharp knife before icing, so that the cake has a perfectly smooth appearance.

Almost daily in my Bureau work I come up against this lack of basic instruction in recipes.

"Why is my short pastry hard?" is a question which I have answered privately to several readers this week.

Had their recipes told them to use merely sufficient cold water to make the mixture hold together instead of saying vaguely "mix with cold water," this difficulty need not have arisen.

"Why do the cherries always sink to the bottom of my cakes?" is another of the popular queries of the moment. The fruit should be washed in warm water to remove its stickiness before it is dried, floured, and added to the mixture. It is inevitable that sticky or moist fruit should disport itself at the bottom of a cake.

The Way To Grill

Grilling seems to cause a certain amount of heartbreak among several readers.

Whether the grill should be hot or cold when the food is placed beneath it is a surprisingly frequent question. As a rule a cookery book will tell you to "place under a red-hot grill." but few will explain that all grills of fish or meat should have oil poured over them (melted butter will do, if you prefer it); that fish should be sprinkled with flour before it is put beneath the grill; and that seasoning must be added after cooking. To season before grilling merely results in wet patches on the surface of the food that will not readily brown.

To-day's Economy Recipes

BEETROOT SOUP

MELT an ounce of bacon fat in a large saucepan, add one large sliced beetroot, three cut-up tomatoes, a chopped onion, a cut-up carrot, and a small piece of cut-up turnip. Cook together for ten minutes over a slow fire and add a quart of stock and half a pound of haricot beans, which have been soaked overnight.

Season with salt and pepper and simmer all gently for two hours. Pass the soup through a sieve, return to the saucepan with a teaspoonful of vinegar, and re-heat.

. . . .

MOCK CHERRY PIE

THIS is Thanksgiving Day, so here is a cranberry recipe from America. Mix together half a pint of cranberries cut in halves, a teacupful of seedless raisins, a tablespoonful of flour, and two tablespoonfuls of sugar. Place this in a pastry-lined pie tin, dot over with flecks of butter, cover with a top crust. and bake very thoroughly so that the under crust is well cooked. Try this—the menfolk all enjoy it.

SOMETHING HOT FOR SUPPER, *Please!*

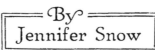
By Jennifer Snow

THOSE chilly, unfriendly week-end suppers with their cold joint and quivering blancmange! No wonder husbands want to boss the home to the extent of demanding firmly something *hot* for supper.

Naturally, the woman who has to cope with the Saturday or Sunday supper single-handed wants labour-saving dishes. But if there is no hot-pot, curry, or shepherd's pie ready to heat up, she

---

The Eternal Question

There's porridge and bacon for breakfast,
Eggs and a cup of tea,
But what shall we have for luncheon?
That's what is puzzling me.

Tea? Oh, that's perfectly simple,
Cake and a scone or two,
But what shall we have for dinner?
What can I give them new?

I know why I'm getting wrinkles,
I know why my hair turns grey,
It's just this eternal question,
What shall we have to-day?
D. A. G.

---

need not resort to the cold remains of the luncheon beef.

Here are some recipes for which the ingredients are likely to be in the larder.

Cheese Pudding

Grate some cheese until you have enough to fill a pint measure, then grate breadcrumbs on the same grater—so that you get the full value of cheese—to make an equal quantity. Grease a fireproof dish, make a layer of breadcrumbs, then one of cheese, and sprinkle with salt and pepper, adding a little made mustard and a suspicion of cayenne.

Continue the layers, finishing with breadcrumbs. Beat two eggs, add to half a pint of milk, pour it over, put dabs of butter on top, and bake for about half an hour.

Cheese Spaghetti

This can be prepared beforehand. Cook your spaghetti in quickly boiling salted water until tender, then drain away the water and add plenty of grated cheese, a good-sized piece of butter, a dash of various piquant sauces, and good seasonings. Heat, stirring occasionally, and make quite sure you have plenty of cheese in the dish.

With Tomato

Use the same ingredients, but make in a fireproof dish with layers of spaghetti and cheese. Heat half a pint of tomato pulp with half a pint of beef stock, adding a clove of garlic and seasonings. Cook for five minutes, then remove the garlic, pour the stock over the spaghetti, and bake in a moderate oven for half an hour.

Savoury Meat

Take the gravy left from lunch, add some tomato sauce or any other piquant sauce, and heat in it slices of cold meat. Flavour with a minced pickled walnut, and when very hot pour on to a dish which has a rampart of mashed potato. Or, if preferred, the meat can be served on a bed of hot boiled macaroni.

Baked Eggs and Rice

Grease a baking dish and put at the bottom half a pint of cooked rice mixed with half a pint of tomato sauce. Break six eggs carefully on to the rice and sprinkle with a gill each of grated cheese and grated breadcrumbs, mixed together. Add dabs of butter and bake in a hot oven for ten minutes.

Picnics Ahead!

By Helen Simpson

HOT weather—let us hope—and a holiday!! Immediately we pack our picnic baskets or fill our haversacks, and rush away to the nearest sea, or to the country, where the harvest is in progress and the heather already purple, and have as many of our meals as possible in the open air.

One gets a little tired of sandwiches, even though there are so many different varieties we can make. What about some patties for a change? Veal, ham, and sausage patties, for instance, or lobster. Then there are little Cornish pasties, Scotch eggs, and home-made sausage rolls.

All these things are delicious, and they have one great advantage over sandwiches—they can be made the day before, and so are all ready to pop into the picnic basket. We all want to avoid that early morning rush of cutting sandwiches to-morrow!

An Easy Recipe

A quarter of a pound of ham, sausage meat, and cooked veal will make ten patties. The ham and veal should be minced, mixed with the sausage and flavoured, and a teaspoonful of chopped parsley added. The mixture should be moistened with a little stock.

Divide the pastry into ten pieces, cut out each piece into a round of about 5in. in diameter, and put a spoonful of the mixture on each. Then moisten the edges with a drop of water, and draw them together, pinching them securely. Turn them over and gently shape them into small buns, making a hole in each and decorating them with little shapes made from the remainder of the pastry. They should be baked in a *hot* oven, and flaky pastry should be used.

Another kind of veal and ham patty is made with the veal and ham mixture to which are added a teaspoonful of grated cheese, a little grated lemon rind, and a level tablespoonful of flour, moistened with a little cream or stock. In this case the sausage is omitted, and the patty cases are already made and hot before the mixture is put in.

Lobster patties are filled with a mixture of good tinned lobster made by putting an ounce of butter in a saucepan, adding flour (a tablespoonful), mixing it smooth and adding, mixing all the time, a quarter of a pint of milk. Stir while it boils for a few minutes, add seasoning, take it off the fire, and add the lobster cut into little pieces. Add a teaspoonful of lemon juice, and if liked a tablespoonful of cream. Fill the patty cases with the mixture.

Making the Cases

The patty cases should be made of puff pastry, baked in a moderate oven. When they are ready, take off the patty cover and put the case in the oven for a minute to dry before adding the filling.

Cornish pasties have as their filling thinly sliced raw potatoes, chopped raw onion, and chopped raw meat, well seasoned. Each square of pastry (about six inches in size) should have a layer of potatoes, a layer of meat, and a layer of onion.

The mixture should be put in the centre of the pastry and the edges brought together and moistened with beaten egg. They should be cooked in a hot oven until the edges of the pastry are sealed, and then cooked slowly for about an hour and a half. Cooked meat and vegetables should not be used.

The pastry is made with three-quarters of a pound of flour, a teaspoonful of baking-powder, and five or six ounces of lard or dripping. Mix the flour and baking powder, rub in the lard or dripping and make into a thick paste with a little water. It should be rolled out to the thickness of about a quarter of an inch.

For sausage rolls use flaky pastry, and add half a cooked sausage to each square of it. Pinch the edges together, and brush over with milk. Make two or three holes in each roll, and bake in a hot oven for about twenty minutes.

Lettuce travels well if it is wrapped in grease-proof paper and then in a napkin or cloth. It should, of course, be washed and crisp before being packed. The small round tomatoes travel best, and they should not be over ripe.

A squeeze of lemon juice on the lettuce is excellent. The lemon should be packed whole in the picnic basket, and not in halves or slices. A few cheese biscuits are also a good addition to the meal.

Fruit should be chosen with care. Plums are too soft to pack well. Small juicy apples and pears are best, and if there is room a tin of fruit is good—but don't forget a tin opener.

For Thirsty People

If possible allow a vacuum flask for each person. Tea is really better if the milk is added later, so take one flask of milk and the rest of tea. Just in case the milk runs out, take an extra lemon, and use a slice of that instead. Russian tea is most refreshing. If you are going somewhere where you know that you can get a jug of water, take some lime juice or orange, grapefruit, or lemon squash, and a vacuum flask of ice chips.

Rock cakes, coconut rocks, and rice buns are better than slices of cake, which are so apt to crumble or get dry.

Don't forget the sugar and salt—and bury or take away all litter such as paper bags, tins, paper plates and cups, and ice-cream wrappers.

Make rock buns for to-morrow's picnic—they carry so well. Note the special wire rack for cooling cakes fitted to the stove in the picture.

Meals at a Moment's Notice

Tinned fruit, cleverly used, makes decorative trifles.

AN emergency meal is not difficult to contrive from a well-stocked store cupboard, if we remember that instead of simply using things just as they come out of their tins, we should combine tinned and fresh foods to make appetising dishes.

Take soups, for instance. Nearly all "ready-made" vegetable soups are made extra good by using milk instead of water; and to improve them still further, try adding a spoonful of cream to tomato, celery, or pea soup just before it comes to table. This is not so extravagant as it sounds in these days when so many people possess the small machines for making cream from butter and milk.

Instead of serving corned beef in a cold lump, try shredding it coarsely, and mixing with chopped cold cooked potatoes, a little onion and an egg, and frying in dripping. Served with poached eggs on top and a sprig or two of parsley, this will seem quite a recherché dish.

Tinned peas can be made to taste like the fresh vegetable if heated in a colander, with a good-sized lump of butter, over a saucepan of boiling water. Asparagus can be used in omelettes, or for dainty tea rolls, and carrots from a tin heated with butter or a little cream will make a useful vegetable dish.

Try mixing tinned and fresh fruit for a fruit salad.

Tinned fruit make excellent trifles, using the juice to moisten sponge cakes, placed in individual dishes, and spreading the fruit on top before adding the custard. Use a few of the berries for decoration.

SPAGHETTI
is No Joke!

SPAGHETTI has been slandered too long. Most people think of it in one or both of the following ways:—

1. As the cheapest thing on the menu.

2. As a joke, the good old joke of a fat man trying to eat it without getting wound up in the coils.

"Oh, it will make you fat," protest the slimming enthusiasts. Probably they have never seen a thin Italian, but there are really a great many—and they all eat it!

Not Mere Starch

Properly treated, it is a complete food. Of course, you must eat lots of butter with it, and grated cheese and a good sauce of tomato and onion and whatever else you happen to have in the house. So it can no longer be called "just solid starch."

It is nourishing, and you mustn't eat bread with it, or potatoes, if you want to keep your girlish figure. But eaten instead of other starches it fills their place and more.

There are those who can go right on to a fillet steak afterwards, but for ordinary appetites a green salad will be enough. I need hardly add that a good red wine makes the meal not only better but celestial.

The reason, I have come to believe, why this great food is so badly treated in England is that few people, unless they have been to Italy, have ever really tasted it. And even if they have been to Italy they probably avoided it as something gross and excessively difficult.

People will serve it on toast, improving neither the toast nor the spaghetti, which should never be served with any other starch.

Don't Wait

Spaghetti is not difficult to cook, but it must be done properly. And it must not wait after it is cooked, or it will go soft and mushy. That is why, in most restaurants—even Italian ones—there is nothing to recommend it beyond the price. It must be cooked separately for each order.

First, you must have a really big pot, the bigger the better. There ought to be at least three quarts of water to a pound of spaghetti, and it should be well salted and boiling really violently before the spaghetti goes in.

It will take about twenty minutes to cook, and in the meantime you are making the sauce, or sugo, the smell of which no appetite can resist.

With Garlic

Start with some olive oil in a saucepan. When hot add chopped onion, parsley, and garlic (unless you absolutely can't stand it—just a little, and you won't regret it, I assure you). Now add tomatoes, or tomato paste, or both. Fresh tomatoes are good, but I really think tinned ones make a better sugo; use lots and let them simmer down a long way.

Salt and pepper, and it's ready; but it will be much improved by the addition of meat stock or essence, or chopped ham, or chicken or chicken livers, or mushrooms, or a little bacon, all finely minced. Taste and see. The sauce really decides the flavour, and can be varied infinitely

"It takes about twenty minutes, and in the meantime you are making the sauce."

at the discretion of the cook.

The spaghetti itself needs tasting, too. Never trust the clock. It must boil violently all the time, and is done when it is still quite firm but is not starchy in the middle. You can tell best by rubbing a piece between your fingers.

Pour it into a colander and drain thoroughly, shaking it so as to get all the water out.

Then serve. It saves time, heat, and trouble, and is consequently better, to serve directly into individual plates; soup plates are easiest when it comes to the eating. Let several lumps of butter melt into each dish; add the sauce on top, and there you are.

Grated cheese, of course, follows to taste. Parmesan cheese is best, but rather difficult to obtain unless you have an Italian store nearby. Gruyère

"Turn the fork away from you, and go ahead. . . . Bravado is needed."

comes next. Do not use a strong cheese; it destroys the flavour.

Of course, macaroni cheese is very good with cheddar, but in that case leave out the sugo and brown the whole thing in the oven in a fire-proof dish. And the French eat boiled macaroni with meat, like potatoes, with meat gravy. It is nice with just butter and cheese, or butter and anchovies and cheese, or butter and capers and cheese; but macaroni sugo is the classic dish, and I think the best.

As to eating it, that takes practice. Turn the spaghetti round your fork, away from you, against the edge of the soup plate, and go ahead. Don't worry about the ends. Bravado is what is needed, and I never said spaghetti was a dainty dish, anyway—I only said it's a good one.   BETTY LANE.

"You mustn't eat bread with it, or potatoes."

PUT SUMMER ON

The... MENU

Give the children plenty of oranges. A big orange cut in half, depipped, cut into sections, sugared, topped with a cherry, and served like grapefruit, is a pleasant addition to the breakfast or dinner menu.

Mix fruit and vegetables in your salads. Apple, chicory, and walnut is an unusual mixture that will be much appreciated.

THE sudden arrival of warmer weather should be reflected immediately upon the week's menus. This is immensely important not only from the gastronomic point of view but for the health of the household. Weather changes, even for the better, mean a certain lowering of vitality, and if on a warm day one is faced with a meal of the stew-and-suet-pudding type one is either disinclined to eat or, having eaten, disinclined for effort and generally "off colour."

The mere substitution of cold meat and plain salad for the usual entrée is not enough. It needs a good deal of thought to get the planning of the household meals out of the cold-weather routine.

Light Yet Nourishing

When arranging meals for warm weather choose food that is nourishing but at the same time light. It is a mistake to omit all nourishing foods, because the languor supposed to be due to unexpected heat is often in reality partly caused by hunger.

The lighter kinds of fish, such as sole, whiting and plaice, should be chosen: well-flavoured shrimp or anchovy patties are good, and, instead of chops and steaks, try sweetbreads (they can now be had quite inexpensively), veal, brains, and, if possible, a little chicken. Small luncheon chickens at 1s. 6d. are good value, and can be served with "trimmings" to make them go further. Here are some useful recipes for hot weather menus.

Veal Cutlets

Have the veal cut very very thin, then pound it thoroughly. Parboil, then cut into round pieces, sprinkle with salt and pepper, dip in egg and breadcrumbs, and fry in deep fat. Drain well, and serve with a fried egg on top of

By Jennifer Snow

each, crossed by narrow strips of anchovy.

Savoury Sweetbreads

Parboil the sweetbreads, and cut into slices. Take a covered dish, and in it put a thinly sliced onion, two chopped chives, a bayleaf, two cloves, salt, pepper and the juice of a lemon, and let the sweetbreads soak in this for three hours.

Then coat the slices of sweetbread in a thin batter, fry a golden brown and serve with fried parsley.

Brains With Piquante Sauce

Scald the brains in boiling water, then cook for half an hour with two slices of chopped ham, a small beetroot sliced, a small chopped onion, a bayleaf, some parsley, salt, pepper, and a gill and a half of stock (or half a gill of white wine, if you have it, and a gill of stock). Serve covered with piquante sauce.

Fried Brains and Spinach

Parboil the brains, and cut into even-sized pieces. Roll these in beaten egg and breadcrumbs, and fry a light brown in deep fat. Drain well. Serve on croûtons of fried bread, with a border of spinach.

Salads, provided they are cleverly varied, can be served at every lunch and dinner. Sometimes they can be arranged on individual plates after the meat course, or substituted for soup. If you have soup on the menu, make an appetising salad as a one-dish course, with any cold meat or fish you have on hand. Cut the meat or fish into convenient pieces, and mix with lettuce, endive, chicory and watercress, plus a good dressing. Put as many ingredients into the salad as you can, and you will find that a little meat goes a long way, and everyone will enjoy the dish.

Apples with Chicory and Walnuts

A good salad for these days is apple, chicory, and walnut. Take a few crisp lettuce leaves, wash them and shake them dry in a salad basket, and arrange in a bowl or on individual plates. Wash the chicory, and chop into dice. Peel the apples (Worcesters are crisp, juicy, and excellent for salads). Arrange the chicory and apples in layers on the lettuce, cover with dressing and garnish with a few peeled and chopped walnuts.

Sweets should be light and above

all appetising. After a salad meal, a sweet omelette is delicious and nourishing. Or try the lightest of cheese soufflés instead. Now that eggs are cheap, soufflés are a reasonable luxury for any menu. Make your jellies with milk instead of water, and serve such things as junkets (coffee, caramel, or chocolate) and fools made with custard and fruit purée.

Whipped Rice

Rice pudding is more appetising if cooked carefully in the ordinary way and when cool removed from the skin and whipped up with a little cream and the beaten white of an egg. Heap in a deep dish and sprinkle with flaked chocolate (drinking chocolate sold in flaked form can be used for this).

If fresh fruit has not already appeared in the salad, serve it at the end of the meal. A good-sized pineapple can now be had for 1s. 6d.

English housewives to-day realise what an ultimate economy it is to invest in a refrigerator. Food is kept crisp and cool, there is no danger of contamination of any sort—provided the inside of the box is kept scrupulously clean—and the provision of iced drinks and sweets is possible at all times with its help.

Pastel Coloured Refrigerators

I have just seen a new and very attractive-looking refrigerator of the ordinary ice-box type. This is 30in. high and 36in. long, and, having a white porcelain top, takes the place of the ordinary kitchen table. It has 5¼ cubic feet of storage space, and, with its primrose-painted "bodywork," is a decorative addition to the kitchen equipment.

This refrigerator-table costs £10 18s. but there is a smaller box-refrigerator, also prettily painted in a range of pastel colours, that can be had for £3 18s. For households where there is electricity, there is, of course, a big choice of mechanical refrigerators, a new "baby" model being priced at £19 10s.

TO-DAY'S French Recipe

OMELETTE MARIETTE

Ingredients

SIX eggs, three medium-sized boiled potatoes, three tomatoes, peeled and freed from seeds (the tinned variety will do), four ounces of butter, and pinch of salt and pepper.

Method

Beat up three eggs on one plate and three on another. Cut potatoes and tomatoes into thin slices and fry in half of the butter, stirring with a fork until partly mashed. Put aside in a warm place.

Now heat a fireproof dish in the oven and put in the remainder of the butter. When hot, add three well-beaten eggs. When these are partly set, spread the vegetables over them and cover with remaining three beaten eggs. Bake in a hot oven until golden brown. This will be sufficient for four people.

The RAMBLER'S FOOD and DRINK

by Claude Fisher

FOOD and drink can make or mar the Whitsun ramble, cycle tour, or camp, as indeed they can any outing, even for the least fastidious of us.

So, whether we elect to cook our feast, or whether we take it with us, it is worth a deal of care.

A favourite method of mine when rambling or cycling is to buy from where I happen to be some fruit, biscuits, and some unsweetened chocolate. For a light meal these are excellent, and a call later for a lager or a cup of tea or other drink completes a welcome repast.

Our British lack of imagination in the sandwich line, more particularly among private individuals, is amazing. Ham, beef, or hard-boiled egg form many ramblers' sole resources, and frequently super-dry and uninviting at that.

ALLURING SANDWICHES

Yes, I am criticising. I feel entitled to after tasting such alluring sandwich fillings as mayonnaise-covered salmon and lobster on anchovy paste; bananas and honey amid brown bread or scones; and pounded and shelled walnuts with cream cheese.

So I counsel you make your sandwiches with imagination. Try toast instead of bread for a change. It is satisfying. A toast sandwich evenly spread with butter to which chopped parsley may be added and with small sardines lying side by side, seasoned to taste, is a meal in itself.

Biscuits, too, such as cream crackers, digestive biscuits, and the like, make tasty and varied sandwiches. So do scones. And here are some more fillings. Gruyère and all the cheeses, especially cream cheese,

which can often form the basis for other ingredients such as chopped gherkins, almonds, salted or plain, sliced apples, red currant jelly, all of which, however, make tasty enough sandwiches on their own. Hard-boiled yolk of egg mixed with creamed celery or shredded onion and sardine are others.

TOOTHSOME MORSELS

Sponge fingers with sweet fillings are toothsome morsels. Try strawberry jam and cream with them, or a fruit mixture.

Here is a jolly one: 1lb. prunes stewed with sugar, ½ gill of cream, ¼lb. almonds and vanilla essence beaten together.

If you must have ham or beef or their kind, salad—green or Russian—sauces of all kinds, pickles and chutneys make good companions.

But there are other solid and not very imaginative fillings: sausages of all kinds, pork and beef, liver, breakfast and luncheon; smoked salmon;

chicken, game, pork, brawn, rabbit, tongue.

The tea-maker in camp or by the wayside will find it worth while carrying a small muslin bag or a square of muslin in which to place the tea and insert it in the pot. Allow for the leaves to swell.

Of other drinks—and the thermos type of flask keeping them hot or cold, as when starting, is a tempting proposition—coffee and chocolate will occur to all.

What about mocha for a change, half coffee, half chocolate, or one of the meat extracts?

Lemonade, orangeade, grape fruit, and limejuice cordial are common enough cold liquids. But have you tried a cider or claret cup or some other cup? Pineapple lemonade is uncommon but good. Half a pint of water and ¼lb. sugar boiled to a syrup with a couple of lemons and a small tin of pineapple grated up will, when diluted, make a pint and a half. But get all the new milk you can when in the country!

He who cooks may read, but he will never cook decently until he practises. No writing can teach him, only guide him.

SMALL FIRES BEST

Let him learn then without unnecessary experiment that the cooking fire should be small and manageable. The ideal is a heap of white hot ashes laid where a turf has been removed and placed aside to replace when finished. For safety sake lay the fire away from overhanging branches, bushes, bracken, stacks, and the like.

Some campers fry eggs on flat stones, but most of us prefer pots. A frypan and two or three nestling pots with handles are necessary for comfortable provision for, say, three campers.

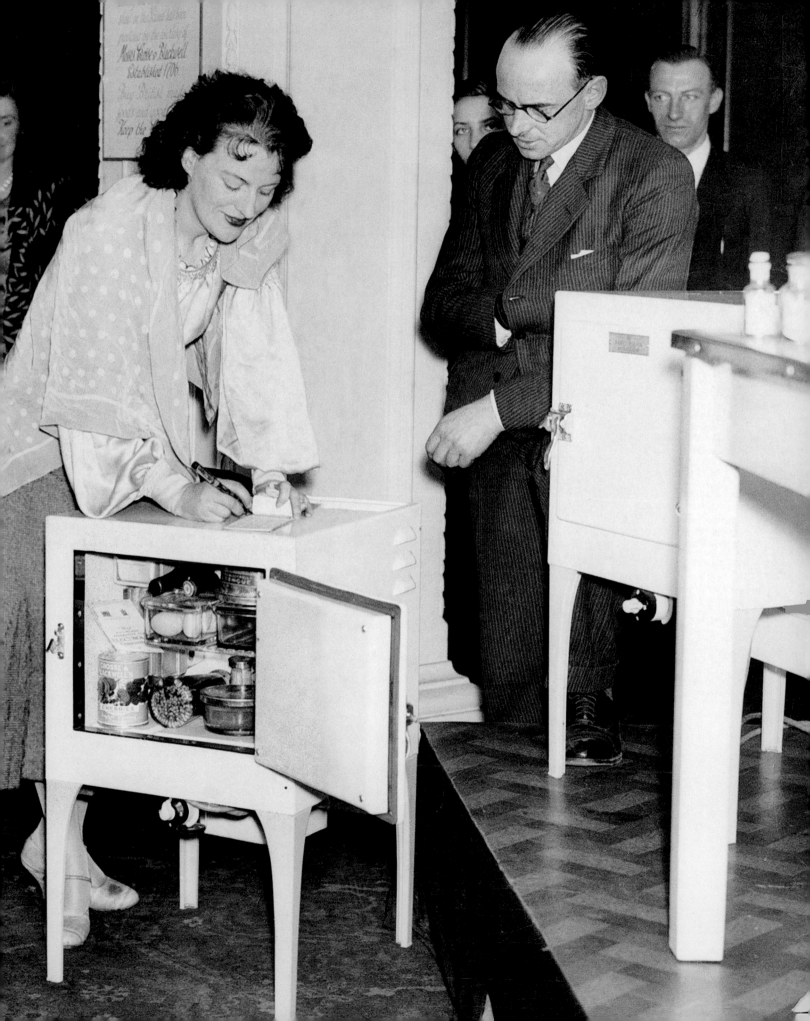

Are You Tired of Salads?

—Then Try Some of these New Ones

By Countess Morphy

SCENE — any British home. Time — any mid-August evening of 1933. Dinner is being served : there is the usual salad-bowl on the table. Says any husband, " My dear, I'm tired of this rabbit-food." Says any wife, " Well, what else can I have this hot weather ? And salads are so good for you, darling."

Of course we're all bored with " rabbit-food " after a whole summer of heat-wave, when salads seem the only possible fare. But salads needn't be just " rabbit-food," by any means. Try something rather special in this line and there will be no more complaints of the monotony of the plain lettuce-tomato-cucumber alliance.

INSTEAD of the usual salad-bowl mixture, Countess Morphy suggests a novel way of stuffing cucumbers.

Apples for a Change

Apples are cheap and plentiful just now and are very refreshing in hot weather. An attractive salad can be contrived by making a neat round incision on the top of an apple, then removing the core without piercing the other side of the apple, removing a little of the pulp, and filling the cavity with fresh gooseberries. Garnish with a few shredded almonds, previously blanched.

Prawns in Cucumber

Cucumber need not be " plain sliced." What about choosing a firm and straight cucumber and cutting it in 2½ to 3 inch lengths? Remove the seeds and some of the cucumber pulp, and fill with chopped prawns that have been mixed with chopped lettuce, seasoned with a little salt and moistened with a little oil. The same can be done with beetroot, choosing the larger kind, and stuffing with some of the beetroot pulp, chopped lettuce and cucumber.

An ordinary beetroot salad is greatly improved by the addition of grated horseradish and a few caraway seeds. The white part of an uncooked cabbage, finely shredded and mixed with dessert apples, peeled, cored, and thinly sliced, also makes a delicious summer salad.

And now that melons are cheap and plentiful, all manner of delicious fruit salads can be made with them. They are very refreshing stuffed with either raspberries or gooseberries, or sliced and mixed with plums or grapes.

All these salads are at their best served very cold. When ice is available they should be put on to it an hour or so before serving.

Cooking at Table

NOT only the bachelor girl in her flatlet, but also the housewife who has to cater for a family of five or six, will appreciate these useful electric gadgets for cooking at table—particularly during the rush hour between rising and racing for the morning train.

The electric toaster and coffee percolator are already too well known to need mention, but one of the

latest breakfast appliances is a gadget which makes toast and coffee simultaneously. The bread is put into a little tray under the percolator and the same heating element serves both purposes.

Another useful table-cooker, containing three small compartments, will make toast, poach eggs, and grill bacon. Although it is quite small and light enough to be lifted with one hand, it is capable of keeping pace with half a dozen healthy appetites.

Then there are various kinds of table cookers which contain a small oven. These are miniature replicas of the standard family cooker, and are intended chiefly for use in the small flat. They can provide a three-course dinner for two or three persons, and are usually installed on a small " dumb waiter " and wheeled to the table when required.   M. E.

25

CHRISTMAS COOKERY

is EASIER NOW!

By Doris B. Sheridan

GETTING ready for Christmas! To the women of past generations this meant hours of kitchen industry, the careful picking over of fruit, the accurate measurement of ingredients, the boiling of puddings, and the baking of cakes.

The old order has changed in so many ways that, wondering whether modernity could infringe upon such an old-established custom as the home preparation of Christmas foods, I spent yesterday visiting the provision departments of several of London's largest stores. On all sides I heard stories of orders for Christmas fare already placed, of demands for cooked puddings and hams, decorated cakes, mincemeat packed in its jars, and—already—for mince pies.

The modern woman has a diversity of outside interests, and at home she is confronted with the problems of small flats and their accordingly minute kitchen accommodation. Who, therefore, can blame her if she goes the shortest way about achieving an end which took her mother, even with excellent domestic assistance, many hours of thought and hard work? A reliable store, supplying goods of first-class quality ingredients, can, at little extra cost, solve her problems for her. Is it to be wondered that she is taking advantage of these up-to-date labour-saving devices?

* * *

AT the same time old customs die hard, and there must be thousands of women cheerfully and pleasurably undertaking the task of preparing all the Christmas fare at home. It is, as in all these matters, a question for personal choice.

The pudding, for instance. You can buy it ready in its cloth-covered basin, requiring only the hour or two of final boiling inevitable before any self-respecting Christmas pudding is ready to appear on the dinner-table. Or you can do the job yourself from start to finish, again making use of a tried and tested recipe.

If this is your decision do not forget that the blended mixture will improve if it is set aside in a cool place under a clean cloth for twelve hours before it is divided among its buttered moulds or basins, and that at least eight hours' steady boiling or nine hours' steaming will be required for the first cooking.

* * *

MINCEMEAT you can acquire in jars all ready for use in such quantities as you will need. If you make your own supplies, remember that the frying of the chopped apple in a little butter improves the general flavour, and, above all, observe the necessity for the air-tight jar.

The actual pies you will, of course, make as you need them. Whatever type of pastry you embark upon, be sparing of the water. Too much water is responsible for many pastry failures. While we are on the subject of pastry, I saw an interesting novelty at one of the stores which would be useful for the Christmas week-end. For a few pence you can buy a nicely browned cooked pastry crust, complete even to the sprinkle of caster sugar, and packed in greaseproof paper in a carton.

With it you can purchase a tin of fruit, and, if you do not already possess one, a standard size piedish to fit the crust. All you have to do is to pour the fruit into the piedish, fit the crust on top, and put the complete pie into the oven for fifteen minutes. Result—fruit pie that will satisfy the needs of four people.

* * *

NOW we come to the all-important Christmas cake. Here again I heard of tons of cakes, iced, adorned with seasonable decorations, and ready for the table, being ordered. Even so, I think the home-made Christmas cake is in a class by itself, and that its vogue will not so readily be relinquished.

From my correspondence I gather that one of the chief difficulties experienced by readers in the making of these large, rich cakes is that of fruit sinkage. This is caused by too moist a mixture, the use of fruit that is not absolutely dry, or by incorrect oven temperature. Cakes with a large proportion of fruit should be put into a hot oven at first to "set" the fruit, after which the heat should be reduced to enable the cake to cook slowly and thoroughly.

It is quite a good plan to stand the tin containing the Christmas cake in a second and larger tin filled with a mixture of salt and sand, as this will prevent the cake from acquiring that too-hard brown crust sometimes resulting from the necessary long period of cooking.

* * *

THE "half-home-made" Christmas cake is another sign of the times. Some people will buy the cake and ice it themselves; others will make the cake and buy the type of prepared icing that requires only to be mixed smooth in cold water before it is spread over the cake. If you make your own icing, remember that hard beating and a little lemon juice produce the white glistening finish which characterises really well-made royal icing.

Then there are the decorations. I saw iced plaques with seasonable greetings; Father Christmas figures with or without the appropriate reindeers and sleighs; robins on tree stumps or pillar boxes; Eskimo children; snow cottages and many other ready-made decorations which obviate any need for proficiency with the icing-bag and pipe.

* * *

GINGER wine, that time-honoured Christmas beverage, is still made by many of my readers. For those who wish to buy their supplies in advance there is a wide choice of wines packed in effective containers of china or glass that could do service as decanters or vases when the Christmas festivities are over.

This "eye to future use" was also apparent in the containers in which some of this season's preserved ginger is packed.

Another good "buy" for Christmas is the cocktail set comprising three bottles in a neat case, one containing salted almonds, a second olives, a third cherries, and the whole rounded up with a bunch of cocktail sticks.

ORDERING Christmas cakes and puddings well in advance—a typical snapshot taken at a London store where a 50lb. Empire pudding is displayed.

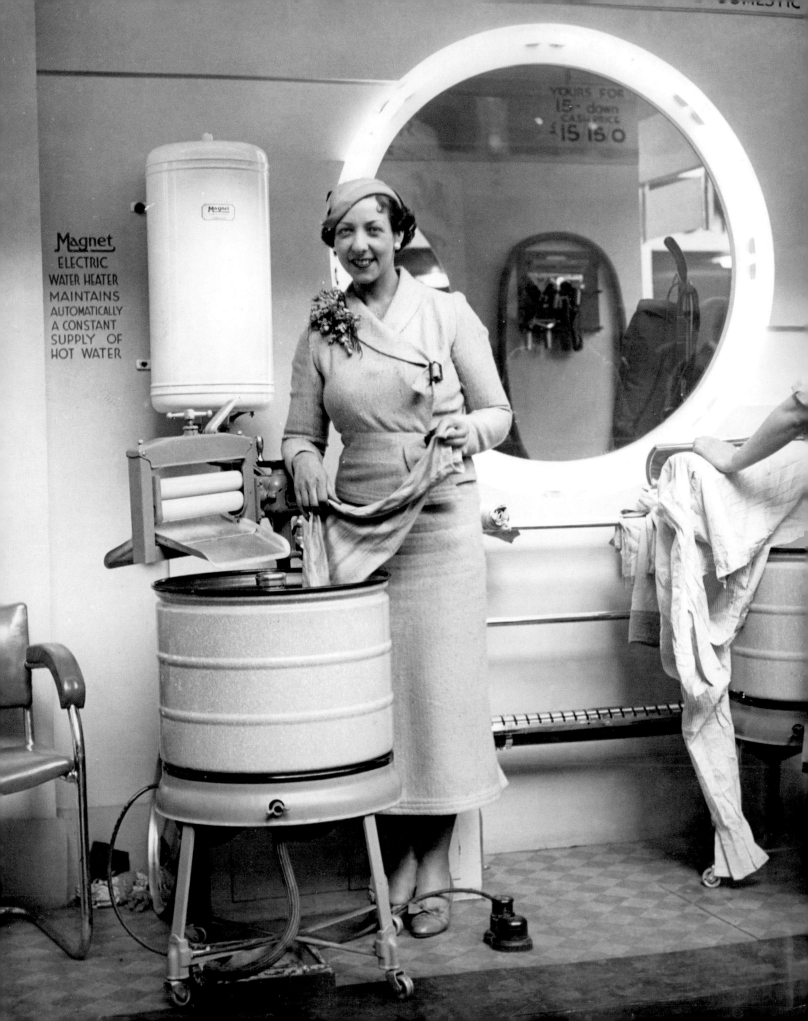

Magnet
ELECTRIC
WATER HEATER
MAINTAINS
AUTOMATICALLY
A CONSTANT
SUPPLY OF
HOT WATER

Household Hints

Imagine - no servants! These are make-do-and-mend suggestions for middle-class wives making the best of life without housemaid or cook. A dirty raincoat? Rub it with hot salt. Stained wallpaper? Use a little French chalk sprinkled on bread. Discoloured linen? Soak it in buttermilk, rinse in water and spread out on the lawn to dry. Preservation and economy are the watchwords: this is not a throwaway society. Beetroot keeps if you add a little mustard to the vinegar; leftover parsnips can be made into cakes and served with bacon for breakfast. Onions can be stopped from sprouting if the root end is held briefly over a flame. Much of this lore is still valid: windows rubbed over with a paraffin rag will repel the flies; sour milk cleans gilt frames; small rooms are made larger by painting skirting boards the same colour as the carpet. Hints that lamp wicks can be made from old felt, and tapers can be made by melting candle ends in a saucer and drawing bits of string through the wax, remind us that electric light was not universal. Apples are as much a staple as potatoes: made into fritters with bacon for breakfast, cooked with brown gravy or stewed into an apple souffle. The luxury item is the refrigerator, newly accessible on a middle class income. It needs to be rinsed inside with a good scouring agent, washed and dried. For households which cannot aspire to a fridge advice is given on how to build a meat-safe.

ANTIQUE FURNITURE, after the polish has been applied on a soft rag, should be rubbed up with a fairly stiff brush, used, of course, in the direction of the grain. This brings up the full effect of the markings on the wood. The same method should be used on oak floors.

* * *

BEETROOT FRITTERS make a welcome addition to the menu. Stew some beetroot until tender, cut into slices, dip in egg and breadcrumbs, and fry. Serve with white sauce and hard-boiled egg passed through the sieve.

* * *

BRASS BEDSTEADS and handles which have become shabby can be made to look like new by painting them over with a special gold paint. This lacquer will last for years without tarnishing. Any rough surface should be removed with sandpaper.

* * *

CANDIED PEEL that has become hard through storing can be softened and made easy to cut if it is placed in a hot oven before use.

* * *

GOLF JACKETS of suède or leather are apt to tear on the shoulder from the friction of the bag strap. Buy some strong adhesive tape, now obtainable in many colours, to match as nearly as possible, and stick the tear together on the inside. If this is done neatly so that the torn edges just meet it will be almost unnoticeable.

* * *

HAM will be found delicious, and rather like the celebrated Virginia variety, if when boiling it you use cider instead of water. If necessary add a little water and place one medium-sized apple, stuck with a few cloves, in the liquid.

* * *

LIVER will not be tough if you fill a small soup plate with new milk, dip each slice of liver into this so that it is completely covered, and lift out and place at once in boiling fat without draining.

* * *

MATTRESSES can be kept from rusting if a little floor polish is applied to the metal parts with a brush.

* * *

MILDEW STAINS can often be removed by moistening soft soap and starch with the juice of a lemon. Spread the paste over the mildew, lay out, and bleach. Afterwards wash in usual way.

* * *

ORANGE SLICES may be used instead of apple sauce as an accompaniment for roast pork. Cut the fruit into thin slices, soak for half an hour in lemon juice, a little sugar, salt and pepper, and place on the pork chops or round the joint. Garnish with parsley.

* * *

SOUR MILK makes a good cleaner for gilt picture frames. Simply rub with the sour milk and dry with a clean duster. This will not remove the gilt, as other methods often do.

* * *

TOMATOES, if unripe when picked, should be placed at once in a drawer and kept in complete darkness for a few days. This will quickly ripen them off, while retaining their freshness.

* * *

VACUUM FLASKS should not be corked when stored after use. Rub the cork all over with common salt to prevent a musty flavour, washing it well before using the flask. If this is done no paper cover will be needed.

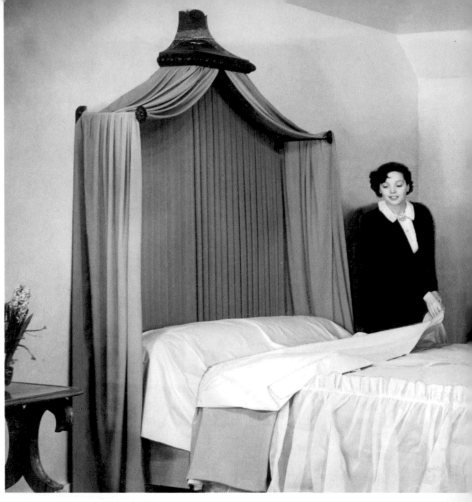

HOUSEHOLD HINTS A B C

LINGERIE SILK should be washed in a solution of lukewarm water and pure soap flakes. Squeeze the garments, rinse out thoroughly in several changes of water, wring lightly by hand, and hang over a line to dry. Do not peg out, and when ironing do so on the wrong side with a cool iron. A hot iron will render the silk fibres brittle, and should never b used.

*   *   *

MAITRE D'HOTEL BUTTER, such a useful accompaniment to steamed or boiled fish, is very simple to make, although it sounds complicated. Mix together with the point of a knife equal quantities of butter and freshly picked chopped parsley, gradually adding a few drops of lemon juice and seasoning with salt and pepper. Keep in a cool place until required. This is quick to make and can save the making of a sauce if in a hurry.

*   *   *

PLANTS grown in pots should always be watered in winter with water of the same temperature as the room or glasshouse in which they are kept. Stand a can of water in a warm place ready for use.

*   *   *

SILK STOCKINGS which have been washed should, when nearly dry, be rubbed with a flannel till all moisture is extracted, when they will not require mangling or ironing.

*   *   *

VEGETABLES left over may be used for Russian salad. Cut the cooked, cold vegetables into dice and spread in a shallow bowl. Add some salad dressing, decorate with strips of beetroot, tomato, or celery, and finish with anchovy.

The Latest Slimming Exercise Is—
HOUSEWORK!

Sweeping and Dusting Your Way to Beauty

[Fanny Inglis.

Does your housework make you slim and supple? It would if you did it in the right way. Compare these pictures—then learn how to get slender while you do your daily dusting.

This is an ideal beauty regime for busy women, who can thus turn the most trivial household task into a slimming exercise.

On the extreme left is shown the right way to dust beneath low furniture, using a long-handled mop. The wrong way to sweep is demonstrated in the next picture.

"I HAVE so much housework to do that there is no time left for slimming exercises," sigh hundreds of busy women.

But actually the very tasks of which they complain can, if done rhythmically and with the correct poise of the body, maintain just that slimness and grace which every woman desires.

Housework exercises are now taught by a London school where women learn rhythm in everyday tasks. Of course, it is essential that each movement should be done in the correct way, otherwise there will be round shoulders, hollow backs, and a general lack of poise.

Even Strokes

The second figure above shows such a common attitude adopted for sweeping that at a glance there appears little wrong with it. But the woman is straining forward, head poking, back hollowed, with her weight thrown heavily on one foot.

Instead, she should be standing almost upright, changing her weight from one foot to the other as she sweeps, moving her broom evenly over the floor in time with a rhythm which she hums as she works. The broom touches the floor at the beginning of each stroke on the beat of the tune, and is never raised far above the floor or stretched out far enough to interfere with the poise of the body.

The right way to polish floors is important. There is usually a strain, lack of balance, hollow back and bent left arm in the wrong attitude.

In the correct position the weight is rested on the left arm so that the right is free to polish the patch in front without undue stretching and without moving the kneeling pad. Again, every movement, even the single twist necessary to put polish on the cloth, is done to rhythm.

How do you mop under low-built furniture? Do you go down on both knees, drop your head almost to floor level, and push the mop vigorously to and fro? Or do you stoop until your back nearly breaks and you hate these new, low pieces?

Forward—Lunge!

On the left is the way to do it. Remember the "forward-lunge!" of your school gymnasium days. This is the same exercise. With the weight on the forward foot, and back and right arm straight, make circular movements until the dust is brought well forward and then fetch it out with short, straight strokes.

And through it all the breathing must be deep, regular, and through the nose, so that no dust is inhaled through the mouth.

When you wash up, don't lean over too far, or, by way of contrast, stand heavily on your heels and push out your diaphragm. Stand easily on the balls of the feet and keep the diaphragm in and the head well poised. Change the pace of the tune you hum according to the state of your crockery, for greasy dishes require slower, more thorough washing. Always wash plates with circular movements *away* from you.

Household Hints ABC

For Your Own Domestic Dictionary

ALMOND MERINGUES are an original party sweet. Make an ordinary meringue mixture, but add to every two whites of eggs 2oz. of ground almonds, folding this very lightly in just before cooking.

- - - - -

BEEF TEA CUSTARD is a nourishing dish for invalids and small children, and makes a welcome change from ordinary beef tea. Slightly whisk two eggs and gradually add a teacupful of good beef tea, stirring well all the time and adding a little salt and pepper to taste. Turn into small buttered moulds, cover with greased paper, and steam until set. Let the custards stand for a minute or two before turning out, otherwise they are liable to break.

- - - - -

COAL FIRES with ugly tiled surrounds may be transformed with a little sheet brass or copper. The brass is cut to the right shape and "sprung" into the sides, and another piece is made to cover the floor-tiles. The total cost of one such renovation amounted to 6s.

- - - - -

FIG SANDWICHES are a popular item for a picnic lunch or tea. Mince some dessert figs with half their quantity of seedless raisins, add some finely chopped blanched almonds, and mix in a good sprinkling of lemon juice. This filling is best with wholemeal bread and butter.

- - - - -

GREASE on coat collars may be removed easily if eucalyptus oil is applied. Rub gently with a soft rag.

- - - - -

IRONS, especially if they have been used for garments that have been starched, should be cleaned before they are put away. Wash them in hot soapy water, to which a teaspoonful of ammonia has been added.

If no starch has been used, the usual rubbing on wire gauze is sufficient to clean the iron.

- - - - -

LACE CURTAINS will last longer if they are placed in a pillow slip before putting them in the copper. This obviates the risk of tearing them when using the copper stick.

- - - - -

ORANGE TEA makes a delicious summer drink when it is iced. Allow half an orange and one teaspoonful of tea to each person. Squeeze the oranges, add ¼ pint of boiling water, bring to the boil again, and infuse the tea. Fill up with boiling water, stand for five minutes, and pour off. Allow to get perfectly cold, and serve with a small lump of ice in each glass.

PIQUE frocks should be ironed on the wrong side to bring up the pattern. Remember to use a slightly cooler iron for linen than for cotton, as it scorches more easily. And when washing out voile frocks ready for the summer, put a little vinegar in the rinsing water and use a very little starch to make the material crisp.

- - - - -

RICE balls for schoolroom puddings can be made in this unusual way. Cook 3½oz. of rice in one pint of milk until tender. Add 1oz. of sugar and chocolate flavouring or vanilla essence. When cold form into balls, dip in beaten egg, toss in breadcrumbs, and fry. Sugar, and serve with custard or chocolate sauce.

- - - - -

STOCK, provided it is strong, can be made into a filling for sandwiches if a little gelatine is added. Then allow the liquid to cool, and it will set into a jelly. Season to taste.

ALMOND LEMONADE makes a change from the ordinary kind, and is an extremely refreshing summer drink. Boil in a quart of water the thinly pared yellow part of the rind of two lemons, the juice squeezed from them, 2oz. of ground sweet-almonds, an ounce of bitter almonds, and ½lb. of loaf sugar.

Simmer for about ½hr., then strain and allow to get cold. It can be served with soda water added, if liked.

* * *

BROOMS AND BRUSHES will not mark the furniture and paintwork if a piece of rubber beading is fixed at the ends above the bristles. Nails with rounded heads should be used, as they will not cut the rubber.

* * *

CARBON PAPERS can be made to last twice as long if the inked side is held before a fire until the surface looks new again. Creases can also be removed if the paper is carefully stretched while it is held before a fire.

EGG SAUCEPANS may be easily cleaned by putting two dessert-spoonfuls of ordinary salt into the pan and rubbing well with a stiff brush. Rinse with hot water.

* * *

FINGER PLATES cut from mirrors are quite as attractive and more practical than those made of glass. As the latter are transparent, it is not always easy to see where they are, while the former not only reflect the fingers, but catch odd lights in the room in a way which makes them very decorative.

* * *

GLASSWARE of the ornamental type will have added lustre if it is polished with a clean duster that has been soaked in paraffin and then dried. This will also discourage flies.

* * *

LAMP WICK can be made, in an emergency, from felt. Cut an old hat into strips of the width required.

MELONS that have been cut into before they are ripe need not be wasted.

Cut some slices about an inch thick, pare off the rind and lay in a shallow glass fireproof dish. Lightly sprinkle with soft sugar, and cover with water to which has been added, and well stirred in, a tablespoonful of black currant jam. Cover the dish and cook in a slow oven, turning the slices occasionally, until the liquid is reduced and the melon nearly clear, like cooked marrow.

This can be eaten hot or cold. Beaten white of egg could be used to top the dish if liked.

* * *

SAFETY RAZOR BLADES which have been used are a useful addition to the work basket. They are invaluable for unpicking machine stitched seams. Keep them in a specially marked box to avoid the danger of cutting fingers. A slotted metal holder can be obtained to take them.

SMALL ROOMS can be made to appear larger by painting the skirting boards the exact shade of the carpet. This increases the apparent floor space.

The photograph shows a room with honey-yellow walls, green hangings and a black carpet, with a black skirting-board to match. Note the little recess where objets d'art are displayed upon glass shelves, and also the plain wooden pelmet painted the same colour as the walls.

NOW is the time to make a Simnel cake for Mothering Sunday. First make almond paste by mixing together in a bowl 1 large egg, 6oz. of ground almonds, ½lb. of caster sugar, and a squeeze of lemon juice. After well pounding together, divide this into two portions, flatten one out on a plate to a round the size of your cake-tin, and keep the other for decorating the top of the cake after it is cooked.

The cake mixture is 8oz. self-raising flour, 6oz. caster sugar, pinch of salt, 6oz. butter, 10oz. currants, 4oz. candied peel, 3 eggs.

Cream together the butter and sugar, gradually add the eggs, which have previously been well whisked, then stir in lightly the flour and pinch of salt, the cleaned and dried currants, and the peel chopped small.

INTO a cake-tin lined with two or three thicknesses of greased paper put half this mixture, then a layer of almond paste, and cover with the other half of the cake mixture. Press it down a little towards the centre so that the cake does not rise in a peak. Cover with grease-proof paper to prevent the top from burning.

PUT into a hot oven, and when the cake has risen, lower the heat and bake slowly for about 2 hours, until a fine skewer or knitting needle comes out clean when pierced through the centre.

Put a band of almond paste round the outer edge of the top of the cake, mark it with a fork, and make little balls of almond paste to put inside this rim. Brush the almond paste with a little beaten egg, and return to the oven until it is set and slightly browned. Turn on to a wire sieve to cool.

A row of cotton-wool chicks and a fancy paper band similarly decorated will give the cake its traditional appearance. This also makes a splendid birthday cake.

ANCHOVIES may be used to make an inexpensive substitute for caviare. Take about six, wash and bone them, and pound them with pepper and salt, a little dried parsley, lemon juice, and touch them with a fresh clove of garlic. Make into a paste with olive oil, and serve on dry biscuits.

BANANAS may be baked in the oven in their skins. Cut off the ends first. When the skins burst take them out, peel them, and serve with sugar, cream, and a sprinkling of lemon.

CANDLES that do not fit the holders need not be shaved with a knife. Dip the bases into boiling water, and they will be found to fit any candlestick.

CORNER CUPBOARDS for the kitchen are obtainable in unstained wood for 37s. 6d. They are six feet high and are fitted to hold brooms and other kitchen utensils. To paint them to match the kitchen décor, sandpaper lightly and apply stain or washable paint.

FISH cooked in a casserole with onions and ham makes a savoury dish. Put into a casserole ½pt. of milk, a little water, one finely chopped onion, a tablespoonful of chopped ham, 1oz. of margarine, and some pepper, and simmer for ten minutes.

Wash and cut up 1lb. smoked fillets of fish, and simmer in the liquid for half an hour. Thicken the liquid with flour and serve with the fish and mashed potatoes or toast.

LINEN may be speedily marked through a copper plate in which the name has been cut in any one of a large variety of types. To brush over the plate, leaving a perfect impression, takes only two or three seconds.

MACKINTOSHES in which a clean rent has been made can be repaired with the adhesive tape used for medical purposes. Carefully shear the edges of the tear, place closely together, put a piece of tape over the join at the back, and press gently with a warm iron.

MATCHES of the non-safety type should always be stored in a tin box, especially if the house is being left for any period. If mice get into the cupboard where the matches are and gnaw at the box there is a risk of its catching fire.

NEWSPAPER AND MAGAZINE TIDIES, made of cretonne or any strong material toning with the furnishing scheme of a room, are extremely useful for holding magazines and papers which are still in use by the members of the household. They are made like an open bag, the width of a chair back, the two top hems being run through with wooden rods to keep the bag stretched taut.

The under-rod is tied at each end to the back of a chair near the top.

ONIONS should be served frequently in cold weather, to prevent colds. Skin and parboil several Spanish onions, take out the centres, and stuff with minced meat, well seasoned.

APPLES that are heavy and, when pressed between finger and thumb, give a slight crack, are the best for all culinary purposes.

BLOTS and smudges on letters, as well as ink, fruit, tea, coffee, and ironmould stains on white and fast-dyed fabrics, may be tackled with this handy pencil, which can be carried in the handbag.

It contains a stain-removing preparation, a drop being applied to the spot from each end of the gadget.

CHEESE dishes will be more digestible if a pinch of bicarbonate of soda is added during the cooking.

ELECTRIC LIGHT CORDS in the kitchen and wherever the atmosphere becomes hot and steamy should be covered with rubber tubing. It is easily put on, and costs very little. Rubbing with a soapy rag twice a month will keep it clean.

GLASS TOPS for dressing-tables or chests of drawers can be contrived by buying inexpensive bevelled glass shelves and "packing" them as panels over lace or silk linings. They will give an individual smartness and are labour-saving.

ICED TEA with vanilla ice cream is a refreshing summer drink. The tea should be made rather stronger than for drinking hot in the usual way. When it has stood for seven minutes pour it from the leaves, sweeten it to taste, and stand in the refrigerator for some hours.

Serve in dainty glasses with a spoonful of vanilla ice cream on top of each.

IRONING at home will be easy if you remember that linen irons best when quite damp, cotton and muslin when somewhat dry, and artificial silks practically dry.

Stockings and flannel pyjamas should always be ironed on the wrong side, as well as all heavy embroideries.

MARROWS are cheap now. To pickle them, take two or three small marrows, 1 quart malt vinegar, one nutmeg (grated), 1 oz. grated horseradish, 1 oz. salt, pinch of cayenne. Peel the marrows, slice in half and remove all the pips. Cut into fine dice. Boil for five minutes in well-salted water.

Drain, and place the vegetable in a preserving pan with the vinegar and other ingredients. Boil again for five minutes. Pack the marrows into the jars, pour the liquid over them after straining, and tie down at once.

PUTTY can be made for domestic repairing purposes by mixing linseed oil with whitening until it is of a workable, doughy consistency.

RED TILED FLOORS will have a deeper and richer colour if a little paraffin is added to the water with which they are washed.

SILVER LACE on uniforms and fancy dresses can be cleaned and brightened by applying powdered magnesia with a brush. Allow to settle for two hours and brush off with a clean brush dipped in spirits of wine.

WILD FLOWERS usually wilt immediately if they are picked in the ordinary way and placed in cold water. But if the stems are put in boiling water as soon as they are picked this will seal them, so that the flowers will last some time. A little salt in the water helps to keep them.

Spring cleaning is the time for renovations. Here are some new furnishing ideas.

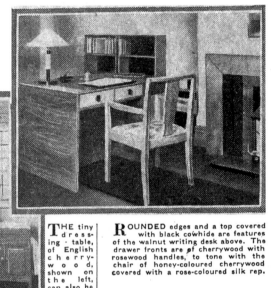

SIMPLICITY of line and an absence of projecting angles are features of the furniture illustrated, which has been designed to take the place of built-in fitments in the small flat. The sideboard above, of English walnut, has been made rather low to accommodate rows of bookshelves above and around it. The low occasional table is also of English walnut.

ANTI-SPLASH nozzles attached to water-taps should be fixed so that the flow of water is directed into the waste pipe. In this way splashing is reduced to a minimum and an efficient flush provided for the waste pipe.

* * *

BATHROOM MATS of crêpe rubber sometimes become hard and curl up at the edges in cold weather. This can be remedied by immersing the mats in warm water until they become soft again.

* * *

BOLSTER CASES on the American pattern are easy to make at home. The under-piece of the case is made the length of the bolster with about 6in. folded in at each end. The top part is made with an overhanging piece. This can be finished with hemstitching or embroidery, and looks well hanging down at each side when the bed is made.

* * *

CRACKLING is more likely to be crisp and brittle if it is rubbed with lemon-juice before the pork is cooked. An additional flavour is given if the crackling is very heavily scored and finely chopped onion, mixed with powdered sage and good seasonings, is rubbed into the interstices before the joint is put into the oven.

FRYING without fat is a good method with chops and steaks. Sprinkle a thin layer of salt in the pan and let it get very hot before cooking the meat for a minute on each side. Afterwards fry slowly for four or five minutes on each side.

* * *

INK STAINS on the fingers can be removed by brushing with a soft nail brush dipped in pure vinegar, and then in salt. The same stains on material should be washed in vinegar and then rinsed well.

LINEN should never be stored in a cupboard near a hot-water cistern or other source of heat. In a warm, dry atmosphere it is liable to become dry and brittle, and even to turn yellow. Choose a cool, fresh place, free from damp, to preserve its whiteness and silky sheen and prevent mildew or discoloration. Linen to be stored for any length of time should not be starched in the final laundering.

* * *

MILDEW ON CLOTHES may be removed in a variety of ways. Rub in damp salt and leave the garment in strong sunshine if possible. Repeat next day if necessary. Or soak the stain in sour milk for several hours and then put it into the sunshine without rinsing. Lemon juice may remove slight stains.

THE tiny dressing-table, of English cherrywood, shown on the left, can also be used as a writing desk. Placed at right angles to the window, it avoids blocking up the light. The sheepskin rug costs 35s.

ROUNDED edges and a top covered with black cowhide are features of the walnut writing desk above. The drawer fronts are of cherrywood with rosewood handles, to tone with the chair of honey-coloured cherrywood covered with a rose-coloured silk rep.

* * *

PICKLED CABBAGE will remain crisp if a small piece of washing soda the size of a nut is added with the spice to the vinegar.

* * *

TULIPS and other flowers with fleshy stalks are often inclined to droop and flag when first put into water. If they are left lying horizontally in cold water overnight the stalks will stiffen wonderfully, and they will remain firm and upright for some time.

Another way is to wrap each head in newspaper from within an inch or two of the end of the stem, and leave standing in a vase all night.

* * *

WASTE-PAPER BASKETS of the wicker-work variety can be painted to match the colour scheme of the room. Wash thoroughly in soap and warm water, and allow to dry perfectly before painting. Use any reliable brand of cellulose paint. Basket chairs may be treated in the same way.

PERMANGANATE of potash or iodine stains can be entirely removed from cotton and woollen materials by rubbing immediately with a cut lemon.

. . . . . .

RUBBER HOT WATER BOTTLES will last much longer if they are washed out once a month with warm water to which a little soda has been added. This should be done whether they are in use or not.

The rubber will keep pliable and will not perish if treated in this manner.

. . . . . .

SATIN SHOES may be successfully recoloured with the liquid dye sold in bottles and intended for straw hats.

Before dyeing, stuff the shoes tightly with crumpled newspaper. Do not

. . . . . .

WINE which is being decanted should have a lighted candle or electric bulb placed just behind the neck of the bottle. This makes it possible to see the first sign of sediment. Stop pouring before this gets into the decanter.

. . . . . .

WOOLLEN COATS and jumpers dry more evenly and keep in better shape if a cane is passed through the sleeves instead of the usual coat hanger. Suspend the cane from the clothes line.

RICE for milk puddings requires about six times its weight in milk. If this point is remembered there is less likelihood of puddings being too dry. Always wash rice in a sieve in plenty of cold water.

* * *

STAINS on the skirting board and the lower parts of furniture are a frequent occurrence when the amateur tackles floor staining during spring-cleaning operations. Keep a bottle of turpentine beside you when doing the job. A quick wipe with a rag dipped in this will immediately remove the stains.

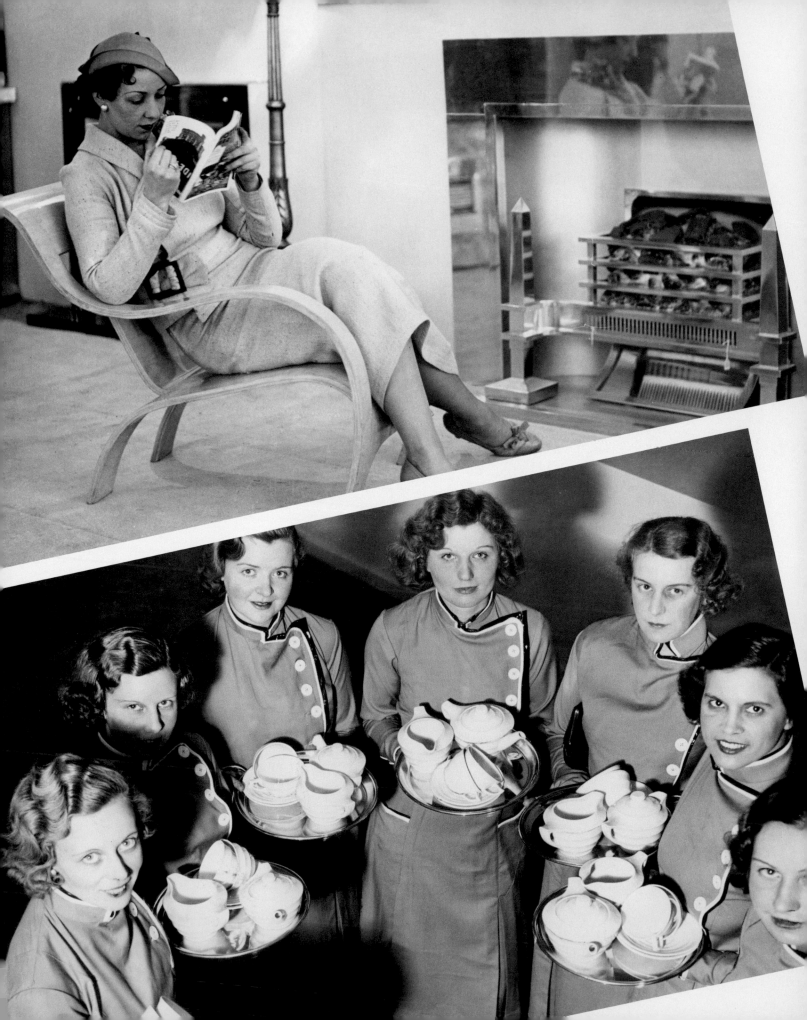

Household Hints ABC

For Quick Reference in Domestic Difficulties

For cold day lunches, vary that well-known dish, "Surprise Potatoes."

APRICOTS (dried) make unusual hot sandwiches. After soaking and cooking till soft, put through the mincer, sweeten, and stew until pulpy. Use as sandwich filling when cold, scattering the bread with powdered cinnamon. Toast the sandwiches on both sides and serve hot.

* * *

BATH TOWELS that are wearing thin in the centre can be utilised to make hair shampoo towels. Fold the towel in half, end to end, and cut a slit up the centre of one half as far as the fold. Then cut a circle, about fifteen inches in diameter, out of the middle of the towel, at the top of the slit.

Bind the edges with tape, thread a draw-string through the circular part, and wear over the shoulders when shampooing the hair.

* * *

CASSEROLES that have been cracked —this may happen if the dish is placed, while hot, on a cold surface—

can be repaired for kitchen use. Clean the casserole with a brush and hot water in which a little soda has been dissolved. Mix thinly a small amount of the best cement, obtainable from any builder or the building department of most stores, and let this run into the crack.

Leave the casserole for a few days to allow the cement to set thoroughly. Afterwards, it can be washed and used again.

* * *

CROUTONS to be served with soup are made by toasting bread and cutting it into dice about half an inch square, which are then fried in deep fat. After being taken out of the fat they should be put to drain in a warm oven or in front of the fire for a few minutes.

* * *

DINNER WAGONS with a highly polished surface sometimes become badly marked by hot dishes. To prevent this, procure some coloured felt, which can be bought in 36in. widths, cut to the size of the shelves and fit in. Choose a colour to harmonise with the dining-room. The decorative effect can be enhanced by appliquéing small circles of coloured felt to each corner

* * *

FISH CAKES are best when "bound" with a good purée of potatoes, consisting of mashed potatoes moistened with milk and butter to form a paste, in which the flaked fish is blended. Paint the cakes with beaten egg, dip in breadcrumbs or vermicelli, and fry very quickly in deep boiling fat from which a faint blue haze is rising.

* * *

MARKING-INK STAINS on white linen should be treated as soon as possible after they have been made.

First soak the marked part of the fabric for a moment in a solution of one pint of water and a half-teaspoonful of permanganate of potash. This will reduce the stain to a brown mark.

Rinse well in cold water and then soak the fabric in a weak solution of peroxide of hydrogen, rinsing this out when the stain has disappeared.

* * *

POTATOES can be made into very tasty little lunch or supper dishes if cooked with eggs as a variation of Surprise Potatoes. Choose large, even-shaped potatoes, and bake them in

their jackets. Cut off a piece at the base to make them stand up, scoop out some of the pulp, drop in a little tomato ketchup and seasonings, then, very carefully, an egg.

Add a dab of butter and a little more ketchup, bake long enough to set the egg and serve with chopped parsley.

Potatoes in the half-shell are cooked in the same way, except that they are cut in half, and all the pulp removed, well mixed with the egg, and seasoned before being returned to the shell.

For spring refurbishing—a delightful new suite in light oak, designed for a small flat, lends itself to a leaf-green and brown colour scheme for a bedroom. Complete with a roomy wardrobe, 5ft. 10in. high and 3ft. wide. Note the attractively shaped frameless mirror.

TO HELP THE CHRISTMAS PREPARATIONS

ALMONDS for the Christmas table need not always be salted. Try soaking them for two minutes in boiling water; then, without blanching, place them on a tray in the oven, and grill them until the skin will rub off easily. Send to table hot in little bonbon dishes without removing the skins.

• • • • • •

BALLOONS for Christmas decoration will blow up more easily and are not so likely to burst if they are first put near the fire to warm slightly and well rubbed between the palms of the hands.

• • • • • •

CHESTNUTS are cheap just now. Try making chestnut cream for a party sweet. Roast about 30 nuts, taking care not to discolour them, peel and skin them, and pound in a mortar. Add enough milk to make a paste, put in an aluminium saucepan, beat together a pint of milk, a knob of butter, 4oz. of caster sugar, and the yolks of two eggs, and boil all together for 5 to 10 minutes. Strain and cool off.

• • • • • •

DUCK OR GOOSE can be made more interesting by using this mixture to stuff it. Cut up the livers and boil with a large onion until tender. Drain off liquid and keep it. Mix the rest with six large chopped apples, half a pint of

breadcrumbs, a gill of stoned raisins, and seasonings, and use with enough of the liquid to moisten.

• • • • • •

ECONOMY COCKTAILS can be made without the usual ingredients and still give a festive air to parties. Use equal quantities of lemon or orange squash (the sort that is usually drunk with ordinary or soda water) and French and Italian vermouth, and shake together. Add a little soda water

CHRISTMAS AT HOME

will be all that you could desire if you watch the "Daily Mail" women's page.

You will find dozens of helpful menus and suggestions for catering and cooking, besides original ideas for entertaining guests of all ages. There will also be useful dress and beauty hints for the holiday.

Read this page every day.

to each glass when it is poured out, and finish with a cherry or a piece of lemon or orange peel.

• • • • • •

HOLLY LEAVES can be frosted for garnishing purposes by first washing well in clear water and wiping with a cloth. Then spread on a flat dish in

a warm (but not hot) place until thoroughly dry. Dip each leaf first into lard that has been melted until it is liquid, and then into caster sugar. Dry well in a warm place and store in tins until required for use. These leaves are not, of course, intended for eating.

• • • • • •

ORANGE SALAD is made more attractive if it is decorated with marmalade jelly dotted round the border of the dish in which it is served.

• • • • • •

PLUM PUDDING SAUCE can be made in this way. Put into a jar ½oz. of caster sugar, the yolk and half the white of an egg, and half a wineglassful of brandy. Stand the jar in boiling water and beat up the contents for 10 minutes.

• • • • • •

YULETIDE CAKES to represent snow scenes are effective and are much quicker to ice than the more elaborate varieties. Instead of putting on the icing smoothly, make it as rough as possible, and when almost set give it the effect of snow by shaking dry caster sugar over it. Finish with a little Christmas figure.

A band of decorated paper, sold for the purpose, gives a Christmas air and saves spending time on the sides of the cake, which are always more trouble than the top.

SUGAR · RICE · FLOUR · SAGO · TAPIOCA · CURRANTS · OATMEAL · TEA · RAISINS · BEANS · PEAS · COFFEE

Suspended from a shelf of blue enamel and stainless steel are (left to right) an apple corer, tin-opener, potato and vegetable masher, potato and fruit peeler, knife sharpener, and cutter for garnishing and shredding. The set costs 7s. 11d.

Below this is an aluminium container with adaptable name disc, 1s., and a collapsible sandwich box, 3s. 3d.

ARTIFICIAL FLOWERS which look bedraggled will be improved if the edges of flowers and leaves are trimmed with a sharp pair of scissors. Then shake over a steaming kettle and allow to dry in a draught.

* * *

BAKED MILK PUDDINGS, such as sago or semolina, are much nicer if sprinkled with grated sponge cake and coconut—a thin layer of each. It will brown beautifully, and has a delicious toasted flavour.

* * *

BLACK SHOE POLISH that is too dry for use should be moistened with a little vinegar. In a household where a great deal of polish is used, it will be found to go farther if slightly diluted with vinegar.

* * *

CARPET SWEEPER brushes should be regularly cleaned by means of a wire brush. Every thread and hair should be carefully removed by this means before putting away the sweeper after use.

* * *

INKSTAINS on silver can be removed by rubbing the stain with a mixture of whitening and sweet oil made into a thin paste. Leave this on for a day, afterwards washing and drying. Finally polish in the usual way.

* * *

LINEN which has become slightly discoloured should be soaked in buttermilk for one or two days. Rinse first in cold and then in warm water, and spread out on the lawn to dry.

NUT BUTTER is a delicious filling for sandwiches. To make it, shell and blanch any nuts, and grind them to powder before mixing with butter. The mixture should be pounded until it is of a perfectly smooth consistency.

* * *

OVEN CLOTHS which will prevent the hands being burnt by hot pans and meat tins can easily be made. Take a double strip, 30in. long and 12in. wide, of a strong material such as hessian or coloured crash.

Sew these two strips firmly together, then sew an additional piece, 10in wide and 4in. deep, at either end, stitching round three sides so that they form two pockets into which the hands can be slipped when removing hot tins from the oven.

* * *

PASTRY will keep crisp for a longer period if it is mixed with milk instead of with water.

* * *

RAZOR BLADES which are too blunt to be used in the ordinary way have many domestic uses, if they are of the perforated type. They can be nailed across loose joins of wood on screens and furniture, choosing an under or back part which is out of sight. This repair is strong and neat.

* * *

REFRIGERATORS need careful cleaning. Remove the shelves and wash these and the inside of the refrigerator with a good scouring agent. Rinse with hot water and wipe perfectly dry. Wash the frame with warm, soapy water, rinse with clean water, wipe, and leave the door open until the whole is quite dry.

Any felt or baize may be washed occasionally with warm soapy water, using a soft nailbrush.

STOCKINGS should be darned diagonally, not in the direction of the weave. They will then "give" more easily and so wear longer. A large hole in the leg of a child's stocking should first be filled in with open net, and patched diagonally, before darning through it.

* * *

SUET will keep well for some days if it is skinned and chopped very finely and then completely covered with flour to exclude air.

* * *

TILED HEARTHS should not be washed if this method tends to split the enamel and glaze. Take a cloth dipped in turpentine and rub them till they are clean. Finally rub with a dry cloth.

* * *

TINS which have become rusty can be restored to their original brightness by rubbing them with a rag dipped in sweet oil and whitening, afterwards cleaning and polishing in the ordinary way.

* * *

VEGETABLES should never be left in the stock-pot or they will spoil its contents. Peeled and sliced vegetables can be added to the pot before it is boiled, but after the stock has been poured off they should be carefully removed from the bones, which can be used again.

* * *

WALLPAPER that has become soiled by dust or smoke can be cleaned by rubbing it over with a flannel dipped in oatmeal.

APPLE SOUFFLE is a light and appetising sweet with which to conclude a hot meal, and can be cooked in the oven while the other dishes are baking. Stew in the oven in a casserole some thinly sliced apples with water, a lump of butter, sugar, and grated lemon rind. Beat to a pulp and mix with the beaten white of an egg, and bake for a few minutes in a greased oven dish.

BEDSPREADS of artificial silk usually have two seams, one on either side. If these seams are covered by a braid about one inch wide, with another length of braid crossing the bedspread at an equal distance from the top and bottom to correspond, a new and fresh appearance can be achieved with very little trouble.

CHENILLE CURTAINS should never be rubbed or squeezed when washed. They should be dipped up and down in a warm, soapy lather made from soap flakes, and left in the water for a few hours. Rinse in warm, slightly soapy water and hang out wet. Press while still damp.

EGG added to soup to make it more nourishing should be beaten first, and the hot soup poured slowly over it. If only the yolk is being used, beat it with a very little milk—then pour the soup over it.

FOWLS that are rather "elderly" can be made as tender as chickens if rubbed with lemon juice, then wrapped in buttered paper. Steam for two or three hours according to size. The fowls may be roasted after being partly steamed.

HOLES in wood which have been caused by nails or screws can be filled up by pressing in a paste made by mixing together fine sawdust and glue. When dry, the surface can be evened by rubbing with sandpaper.

JAM SPONGE ROLLS will not crack in cooking if this method is followed. Remove the sponge from the oven and turn out on a clean, damp cloth. Trim the edges, spread with jam, and roll up quickly.

KNIFE HANDLES that have become stained can usually be cleaned by rubbing with a piece of damp flannel dipped in table salt.

MIMOSA is far less likely to lose its fluffiness if, immediately it is bought, the stems are scraped for an inch or so from the ends and then plunged into boiling water for two minutes. Then put them in water in the usual way. The flowers should thus remain fluffy for several days.

NAILS driven into plastered walls usually become loose as soon as any object, such as a heavy picture, is suspended from them. They can be rendered perfectly safe and firm by this method. Drive the nail into the wall, remove it, and fill the cavity with a mixture of plaster of paris and water. Place the nail in this paste so that it will harden round it.

PANS which have been used for frying fish or onions frequently retain a slight odour. Swill them round with water and vinegar after scouring, and this will disappear.

VARNISHED FLOORS which are to be restained must be thoroughly cleaned before any fresh stain is applied. To remove the old varnish, wet the boards with a solution of strong and hot soda water. Allow it to soak well in, then scrub hard the way of the grain. Rinse with clear, warm water. If any obstinate patches remain rub these with fine sandpaper.

WASHABLE DISTEMPER such as may be purchased dry or ready mixed for use dries quickly and hardens. To obviate this the bucket containing the mixture should be placed in a larger one containing boiling water. The rising steam will keep the distemper smooth and liquid while the walls are being covered. Do not wash the walls until three weeks after the application of the distemper.

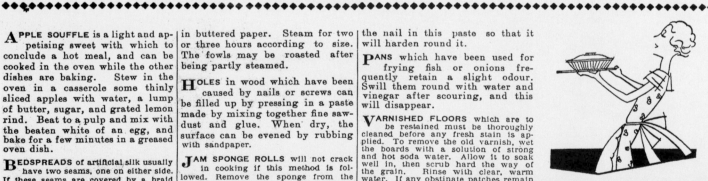

Here is a useful stainless knife which will cut grapefruit or oranges into neat portions ready for serving at breakfast or dinner. Its price is 2s.

HOUSEHOLD HINTS ABC

MANY "Daily Mail" readers have already contributed tried home hints to this useful Wednesday feature. Why not send in your labour-saving ideas? The payment for each hint published is Five Shillings. Address your letter or postcard to The Editress, "Daily Mail," Women's Page, Northcliffe House, London, E.C.4.

IF you are "moving house" this month you may have to cope with the problem of the ugly Victorian fireplace. Here you see how the fireplace in an old-fashioned house has been modernised at very little cost.

The fire surround, which includes a marble mantelpiece, has simply been boxed in with plywood and fitted with an up-to-date fire. A fitment of this kind could be made by any joiner. The colour scheme is grey, green, and silver, a modern washable wallpaper in light pastel green being used for the background, the fireplace itself being painted a soft grey. The "steps" at each side of the recess are laced with silvered metal, which reflects the light of the fire and gives a warm, glowing effect.

AMMONIA should be added to the soapy water in which washleather gloves are washed. A few drops are all that will be necessary, and will keep the gloves perfectly soft.

* * *

BACON for boiling will have a better flavour if a dessertspoonful of vinegar is added to the water.

* * *

CARPETS or mats can be prevented from curling by applying some very thick starch on the edges. Place a piece of brown paper over the starch and iron dry with a fairly hot iron.

* * *

COOKING SALT will crush more easily if the block is allowed to stand on cold tiles, or on a stone sill, for half an hour beforehand.

* * *

FIREPLACES of unglazed red bricks which have become darkened by smoke can be cleaned by scrubbing with undiluted vinegar, using an old nail brush, or similar brush, for the purpose.

* * *

HORSERADISH SAUCE, added to scrambled egg or spread on the toast on which poached eggs are placed, give an excellent flavour. Warm the sauce before using.

* * *

HOUSEHOLD LINEN can be quickly mended by machine. Fill the shuttle with a medium darning cotton and thread the needle with No. 40 or 50 cotton. Machine to and fro over the hole until it is filled in, keeping the needle down and raising the foot at the end of each row.

* * *

INSOLES for shoes, so frequently needed for children, can be cut in an emergency from an old felt hat.

* * *

IVORY KNIFE handles will be freed from stains if they are rubbed with a rag or leather dipped in warm soapy water, with a sprinkling of pumice-stone powder. Polish finally with a clean cloth.

* * *

LEMONS will keep for a very long time if they are put into a basin of cold water. Be sure to change the water every day.

* * *

MERINGUE can be prevented from falling if enough cream of tartar to cover a sixpence is added to the half-beaten eggs. Continue to beat until firm and bake in the usual way.

* * *

ONIONS will not sprout when stored if the root end is held for a few moments over a flame or singed with a hot iron.

* * *

PASTRY left over from making tarts, pies, and so on, can be utilised for making delicious little tit-bits. Roll the small pieces out thinly, spread with sugar, and sprinkle with cinnamon. Form into a roll, cut off into short lengths, and bake.

* * *

RICE for curries will be dry and flaky if it is boiled as follows. Put a breakfastcupful of rice in a large saucepan with plenty of boiling salted water. The water will cease boiling for a few seconds, but as soon as it again is on the full boil, cook the rice for *exactly 13 minutes.*

Pour it at once on a wire sieve, and put it under the cold water tap for a few minutes, stirring it well with a spoon. Drain, and warm up in the oven.

* * *

STALE BREAD will be improved if placed in a steamer over boiling water and allowed to steam slowly from fifteen to twenty minutes. The result will be a very light loaf. This is more effective than reheating in the oven.

* * *

SUN BLINDS should be cleaned before they are put away. If they are made of glazed cotton they should be rubbed over with bath brick and sponged with a rag soaked in warm, clear water.

If they are really dirty, they should be washed in a good soapy lather, rinsed well, starched, and ironed when damp. Allow to dry before putting away for the winter.

* * *

TIES not kept in a tie-press can be kept in order by a simple device. Take pieces of cardboard a little more than a quarter the length of a tie and as wide as its widest part. Double the ties, fold them over this piece of card, and snap two elastic bands round to keep them in place. Two or three ties can be kept on each piece.

* * *

VANDYKED GEORGETTE NECK-WEAR, lace edgings, and all fancy-bordered lingerie etceteras will have a professionally laundered finish if you pin them out flat on a clean pillow to dry. Stretch and secure the spiked edges firmly, and when they are quite dry press them lightly with an iron that is barely warm. A hot iron should not be used, as it will press out the crêpe of the georgette.

* * *

VEGETABLE MARROW is sometimes overboiled so that the pieces break when strained. If this happens it looks better and tastes excellent if the vegetable is mashed with butter, pepper, and salt. Be careful to drain away as much water as possible before mashing.

FINGER-TIP BEAUTY

WHEN using a nail brush to clean the finger tips, use it also lightly on the cuticle and round the side of the nails. Then brush the hand and wrist to stimulate the circulation and improve the colour of the skin.

Rub hand cream at night from the tips of the fingers down to the wrist, working it in with the same movements as you use to ease on gloves.

Cuticle remover is effective in taking away stains on and under the nails, particularly those made by cigarettes. Apply it with cotton wool, and rub gently.

Rinse the finger tips and dry them thoroughly before applying polish, or it will not give an even appearance. Apply it in long strokes from the base to the tip of the nail.

Manicure polishes and other preparations can be obtained in scents to match one's other perfume.

Fashion

In the late 1920s and early 1930s, fashion responded to the Depression by becoming more sober. Rejecting the glitzy fabrics and decorations of the Flapper decade, women avoided conspicuous display in favour of a new simplicity. Instead of jewelled bangles, leather belts with metal motifs were worn by the young. Studs replaced long earrings. Belted jumpers with plain sleeves were regarded as chic, and glittering jewellery was replaced by simple pearls. Black and white were in vogue - long black high-necked dresses in streamlined satins and silks which were slinky but unflattering to women's curves. In the autumn of 1932, the Daily Mail's fashion editor, Victoria Chappelle, declared "Blouse Jackets are Trumps". To compensate for the severity of the tight-fitted evening wear, gowns were almost backless, a hugely tantalising combination. Another way of relieving the severity was trimming with fur, in the days when every wild animal was fair game for the dressmaker. Monkey fur was much in vogue; so were antelope gloves and ostrich feather boas: they looked good against velvet hats and dresses. Men had their own revolution: not so much the lighter fabrics and louder patterns, in the 'gangster' style of American movies, but new elastic yarns which held up their trousers without needing braces.

WHAT YOU WILL WEAR
this AUTUMN

Leading Lines from the Paris Dress Shows. Sketched by ODETTE

FASHION *Puts Your* COAT on the Sliding Scale

By
Victoria Chappelle

Here is a version of the three-quarter coat, in pearl grey wool crêpe, with coral red striped scarf-collar and trimming, and four buttons placed below the waist.

MOST readers who write to the Women's Bureau asking me for suggestions for their spring outfits are, I find, worried about the length of coat or jacket. Shall it be long, hip-length, or three-quarter?

The truth is that dressmakers have put coats on a sliding scale this season. There are all the orthodox lengths, including full, three-quarter, and hip-lengths, with a few others which are betwixt and between, such as five-sixths and seven-eighths. The waist-length jacket this year is not prominent, except for the evening. It is improbable that we shall see much of the odd lengths outside the salons, but the first three I have mentioned may be safely taken for granted. The long coat is made on princess lines or belted, the three-quarter coat usually hangs from the shoulders, while the hip-jacket varies considerably.

This snappy sports ensemble is of mouse grey wool, the hip-jacket fastened below the waist with metal clips. Note rolled collar and woollen gloves to match.

Fashions *about Town*

THE opening of the London season . . . and a sudden outcrop of the very latest summer fashions in theatres, restaurants and clubs! Here are a few snapshots:

At the theatre—a white piqué dress, accompanied by one of the new collarless, wide-sleeved Eton jackets in garnet-red velveteen. Worn with a posy of piqué flowers. (See sketch.)

• • •

A watch as a bag fastening, protected by a plate of thick crystal which magnified the face and the hands.

• • •

A sailor hat of natural chip straw, which had a square crown rising to a curious blunt point in the centre, and a slightly down-curving brim. Worn with very trim, short hair and set off by pearl-stud earrings, this looked very tailored and chic.

• • •

One of the new ribbon turbans showing the hair at one side. Undoubtedly smart, it was apparently a great trouble to put on. At a matinée the wearer had absent-mindedly removed it and was looking at it in despair. "This means I must spend twenty minutes putting it on again." she said to a friend.

• • •

Several white turbans, with accessories to match, which seems to suggest that white is going to be as fashionable in London as it is in Paris. Short white crochet scarves are much in evidence.

HANDBAGS: *Slim Lines and New Materials at the British Industries Fair*

THE new simplicity in fashion means that great stress is laid on the right accessories. And of these accessories the handbag is one of the most important.

Thousands of new handbag designs are on view at the British Industries Fair. Most of them are severely plain in cut and irreproachable in workmanship and finish. The envelope shape is neglected in favour of the top-opening, which is usually of plain chromium. Sometimes there is a snake-chain of silvered or gilt metal, sometimes the convenient thumb-strap at the back, and sometimes the simplicity of the line is broken by no handle at all.

Below are shown a chromium - frame bag of red patent calf, with black composition ornament, and belt to match; navy calfskin bag with light

BLOUSE JACKETS ARE TRUMPS
this Autumn

By VICTORIA CHAPPELLE

BOTH these evening blouses have the new high necklines in front and deep décolletages at the back, but while the model on the left has the new basque and a cape effect, the other is finished with sash ends which tie below two ornamental buttons. Satin, lamé, or velvet would be suitable materials.

A HIGH neck completed by a bow tied behind the shoulder and a broad belt above the basque are distinctive points on this velvet afternoon blouse.

MOST of us are looking round now to see which of the new fashions will help us to face these early autumn days. It is too early for a coat, and a suit does not altogether fit in with one's still summery mood. The solution of the problem seems to be found in one of the new blouses which, shown in the recent collections, have made a tremendous hit in Paris, and are particularly becoming to the Englishwoman. Made on the jumper principle and worn with a trim skirt, it is responsible for the success of the whole outfit.

❖   ❖   ❖

ACTUALLY these blouses suggest very light jackets, and as such must be almost semi-tailored if they are to be effective. Many of them have the new high necks (or can be given one by means of a scarf), which makes them smart for morning.

No flimsy materials are used; velvet is very popular, not only for afternoon but occasionally for morning. The old-fashioned striped velvets, as well as various patterned velvets, may be chosen.

❖   ❖   ❖

FOR the woman who wants a blouse for practical wear, the most sensible choice, of course, would be a light-weight woollen in a plain or fancy weave. Newer than a deliberate match would be a top in a lighter shade than the skirt—especially if one of the new blackberry or mulberry colours are chosen—or in a deliberate contrast. The hat, and perhaps the bag, should match the blouse, but the shoes and gloves will look best if they tone with the skirt.

This gives us the opportunity to try out the effect of the new short basque which is fluted only over the hips, leaving the back and the front quite flat. If this does not appeal to you, the blouse can be made to fit over the hips with a plain belt.

❖   ❖   ❖

FOR the afternoon moiré is a good material, and satin has become important again, but although these blouses may have short sleeves and more elaborate necks, they are always on the plain side.

Quite an attractive neck line for a blouse of this type is achieved by simply inserting a couple of broad bands into each side of a fairly low-cut "V"; these are crossed, so that a slight cowl effect is given just beneath the chin, and the ends set into the blouse itself and buttoned together at the back.

❖   ❖   ❖

SHOULDERS are not exaggerated so much this season —those tremendous frills have vanished—but a slight fullness can be concentrated at the top of the armhole if this suits you. Newer than this, and usually more becoming, is the distribution of fullness between shoulder and elbow in such a manner that it produces a modified pouch, or a series of small ridges or points. But if a plain sleeve is more becoming, do not hesitate to choose it—the collar and, if you want them, some attractive buttons will give you all the elaboration needed.

❖   ❖   ❖

LONDON FASHION SECRETS

Practical Autumn Clothes from English Salons

BY ODETTE

L ONDON dress houses are now preparing the collections of autumn and winter models they will show during the next month. From the advance information which I have obtained I can see that British designers will reveal many fresh and fascinating aspects of the new mode, other than those stressed in Paris. This is stimulating news.

Attractive and at the same time practical ideas are dominant in the minds of the London dressmakers.

I note among the leading features of their forthcoming shows :—

Light-coloured cloth or woollen jackets over dark velvet dresses.

Separate capelets, with buttonholes which make use of buttons on the jacket or dress.

Very tailored-looking pinafore skirts that finish at a high waist-line at the back.

High, loose collars.

Important but not grotesque sleeves.

Touches of fur on cloth or silk dresses to match the coats worn with them.

The toilettes shown in the sketch give an idea of the originality of line and treatment to be offered by English houses. On the extreme left is a dark brown corded velveteen dress with a white flannel jacket, suitable for early autumn wear.

Next to this is a costume with a high-waisted pinafore skirt in dark and light grey check, a jacket in plain grey cloth with checked sleeves and a separate capelet that fastens at the back and is kept in place in front by five buttonholes which fasten over the buttons of the jacket.

Behind this, one sees a plain black marocain dress, and a back

view of the ruby velvet jacket that is worn with it. The next illustration shows the dress of a travelling or everyday costume that is completed by a knee-length cape (not shown).

The seated figure at the extreme right wears a velvet afternoon dress with the loose, high collar that is to be a feature of next season's modes, and rather important looking sleeves in which all bulk is concentrated between a low shoulder line and just below the elbow.

The remaining model is a cloth dress with a touch of fur to match the coat. This coat has a loosely draped collar that hangs away from the neck.

STRANGE FRUITS come to TABLE

A LL SORTS of queer fruits from abroad are now being sold in this country. Many people ignore these unusual things because they do not know how to serve them.

PASSION FRUIT.—The simplest way is to cut off the tops and eat it with a small spoon, rather like an egg. Another way is to scoop out the pulp, mix it with sugar and whipped cream and pile in individual glasses. A few passion fruit added to fruit salad give an unusual piquancy. The juice will make cocktails more intriguing.

CUSTARD APPLES.—Eat the white pulp with a spoon, taking out the large black pips, and adding sugar if liked. Mangoes are eaten with a spoon, too.

AVOCADO PEARS.—For a salad, remove the peel and serve on lettuce with French dressing. Mash the pulp with lemon juice and cayenne for an unusual sandwich filling, or serve as an hors d'œuvre by removing pulp from half shells, mixing until smooth with oil, vinegar, salt, and cayenne, and returning to shells.

POMEGRANATES.—The best way to peel is to cut a small round piece from the top, and then carve down the hard rind in its natural segments, so that the fruit can be pulled apart. A compôte can be made by removing the seeds from some large pomegranates, putting these in a glass bowl and sprinkling with rose water. Make a thick syrup from the juice extracted from one or more pomegranates with sugar to flavour and an equal quantity of water. Heat until it thickens, let it cool, then pour over the fruit in the bowl. Cape gooseberries can be served in compôte, too.

How I Spend My Dress Allowance

Prizes of Three Guineas, Two Guineas, and One Guinea are offered for the best individual dress budgets by readers. Make an account of your own expenditure, write down in 100 words or less your reasons for making any *one* of the purchases mentioned, and send it to "Dress Budgets," *Daily Mail* Women's Page, Northcliffe House, London, E.C. 4, so that it reaches this office not later than by first post on Monday, November 16. Winning budgets will be published, but only the initials of the senders will be printed. The decision of the Editress must be accepted as final.

By a GIRL OF TWENTY

FIRST YEAR.			
Winter coat with fur fabric collar	3	19	11
Tweed coat frock to tone	0	19	11
Stockinette jumper suit	1	10	0
Fur felt hat	0	12	11
Sports beret	0	2	6
Proofed gaberdine coat	2	10	0
Evening frock and coatee	2	10	0
Shantung frock	1	9	0
Straw hat	0	10	0
Linen hat	0	5	0
Cotton frocks	1	0	0
Silk washing frock with coatee	1	10	0
Bathing suit and holiday accessories	1	0	0
Stockings	3	0	0
Shoes	3	3	0
Gloves	0	15	0
Handbags	0	15	0
Scarf	0	2	11
Underwear	3	10	0
Odds and ends	0	14	10
	30	0	0

SECOND YEAR.			
Harris tweed coat	2	17	9
Cardigan suit to match	2	2	0
Velvet evening coat	1	10	0
Tweed skirt and pullover	1	0	0
Velour hat	0	10	0
Wool georgette coat and frock	3	0	0
Straw hat to match	0	12	11
Shantung frock and jacket	1	19	0
Shantung hat	0	10	0
Artificial silk frock	0	13	9
Washing silk frock and jacket	1	10	0
Tennis frock	0	10	0
Tennis shoes	0	5	0
Sports coat	0	9	6
Beret	0	3	11
Two pairs shoes	2	2	0
Evening shoes	0	12	11
Stockings	3	0	0
Gloves	0	15	0
Handbags	0	15	0
Underwear	3	19	11
Odds and ends	1	1	4
	30	0	0

JUST over a year ago I was given my own dress allowance for the first time. It is £30 a year. I spent a great deal of time during my lunch hours exploring the shops in town to find out how much clothes cost, and I bought very few at first because I was not sure what would be most suitable for business and "grown-up" life in general.

I have had time to decide what kind of clothes I need and like most, and I have planned out my complete budget for two years. The second supplements the clothes I have left over from the year before. My winter coat is still quite good, for I bought one with a fur fabric collar so that the material should be the best possible for the price.

I shall buy a good tweed coat, and as soon as the sun shines early in the year I shall buy a spring outfit, and my winter tweed suit will be cleaned and worn by itself. After watching how other girls dress I have decided that the most important thing is to match up one's clothes perfectly, so I try to buy a coat and frock at the same time.

Cotton frocks seem to be of little use except for tennis and holidays, for I do not like to see them in an office. So I buy sleeveless silk frocks with a little coat to match, and then I can wear them on almost any occasion. I am very careful to buy only materials which will wash well.

Made in light-weight tweed gaberdine, this 19s. 11d. frock is ideal for office or house wear. The wide revers soften its otherwise severely trim cut, and a lingerie front can be inserted. Buttons decorate the pleated skirt.

One of the prizes of the bargain hunter with a small dress allowance is this evening gown and jacket for £2 10s. It is made in apple green georgette over a silk slip, and the fashionable elbow sleeves of the jacket are trimmed with black fur. The line is simple, the neck being round, and the skirt, which fits closely at the hips, fully flared.

CLINGING HATS—of Elastic!

LUXURIOUS curls and the newest hats are not friends, by any means, unless the curls can be arranged to stay outside the hat instead of being tucked within. So consult your hairdresser before you visit your milliner! As a matter of fact, these new hats not only cling to the head like a burr, but have a mysterious way of shrinking to half their normal size the moment they are removed from the head. And the reason is quite simple—they are made of elastic.

• • • • • • • •

But from their appearance you would never guess it. The material which is used might be a plain chenille fabric or a crêpe with a contrasting outstanding rib, but beneath, cunningly woven, are the fine elastic threads which put this type of hat among the novelties of 1933.

It is this elastic which makes it the ideal headgear for any kind of spectator sports as well as for cruising—in not too hot weather—and for holiday wear. Nothing less than a storm or a cyclone, it seems to me, will remove it.

MATALASSE silk and little white plumes are used for the hat on the left, which is ideal for those occasions when everything depends on correct accessories. The helmet shape gives a touch of formality, and the plumes which bind the brim and spread over the crown accentuate it.

Twisting to a gnome-like point atop of the crown, the model in chenille on the extreme right is another version of the elastic cap. A turned-up cuff above the forehead softens the line. These elastic hats can be arranged on the head to suit the individual wearer.

HAIR MODES
go GREEK

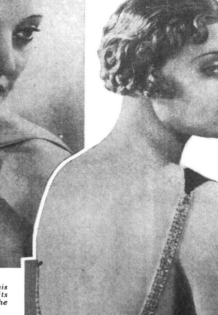

Here is the Jane Austen coiffure, modestly hiding the ears with perpendicular rolls, but revealing the young and lovely forehead. Note the centre parting here and in the first picture. (Antoine).

Very "Greek and Gladys-Cooperish is this elegant coiffure for the evening, with its crowning roll of curls and its emphasis on the pretty ear.

DAY COIFFURES remain simple, but in the evening your hair should be your crowning glory.

You can have your own hair set in the Grecian manner, or if you prefer it you can buy detachable rolls and curls for evening "wear."

Lacquer is less in evidence than it was last season.

Specially designed for the woman with unruly curls is this smart sculptured hairdressing, breaking into becoming waves on the forehead.

WHAT'S NEW *for* CHRISTMAS

A HUGE bronze hairpin — the newest gadget for holding the woollen sports scarf in place. Very chic.
....

Bracelets made of three strands of large glass beads, in the rich velvet tones of wine, amethyst and ruby.
....

Chromium manicure set on a stand; needs no cleaning. Also nigger leather pochette fitted with enamel powder case. Christmas presents that are useful and attractive.
....

Evening belt in plaited silver with coral-colour ring and bar fastening.

A new version of the hair-band in flexible gold. Would be chic with a dark fur wrap for theatre wear.
....

Long mittens in black and white net with ruffled tops, also in white satin and fur cloth. Wearing these mittens you have all the "finish" that only long gloves give, and can still show your lovely rings.
....

Bag in black enamel and chromium—very new and unusual. Will be smart with a "classic" tailor suit.

By Our Shop Detective

Shoulder flower in red fish-net and black organdi—a gay touch on a black satin dinner-dress.
....

Dressing gown in flame chiffon velvet, cut on severe tailored lines.
....

Evening bag made like an old-fashioned knitted purse in gold tissue sewn with rubies, contrasting with a flat square pochette in gold kid.
....

Brown suède belt with big square buckle in dark and light unpolished wood; another brown suède belt has a heavy steel fastening like a curb-chain. Either of these would look good on a beige corduroy sports ensemble.

DRESS·SHOW NOTEBOOK

By
Victoria Chappelle

MOST women will like the new short, fitting jacket shown everywhere in Paris. One house is making them in old-fashioned striped silk with plain cloth skirts, and there are some charming models in black sequins worn with black woollen dresses with sequin trimmings. There is hardly a designer who has not seen the possibilities of evening jackets in gold lamé, and there are several quilted models.

It is doubtful whether the jackets with fur sleeves or those with contrasting material sleeves will find much favour, but there were some with a plain back and sleeves allied to a striped front which not only had the charm of novelty but were becoming into the bargain.

* *

CAPES are by no means dead, although they are hip-length instead of shoulder-length now—not that this makes them easier to wear! Interesting evening wraps by Lelong are made on the lines of Florentine cloaks, with a slightly draped hood at the back, a little fitting bodice beneath, and long, fur-lined slits for the arms. A little green brocade 18th-century jacket matches the brocade top of a black satin Mainbocher frock, and Schiaparelli shows a circular cape of her new padded silk mounted on crinoline. This has a tiny upstanding collar with close-set buttons from neck to hem. Raccoon fur is used for the skirt of another of her evening cloaks, which has a bodice of white padded silk.

* *

EVENING silhouettes provide contrasts. Lanvin has a black velvet gown falling off the shoulders, with a broad silver stitched lamé bertha, a fitting bodice, and a wide skirt gathered at the waist. On the other hand, Mainbocher shows slim princess gowns cut to a point in front and disclosing a hem of pleated

net or lace, the décolletage outlining the bust. Another house shows straight tube dresses, spreading at the hem, while Chanel has a bewildering variety of outlines.

Trains are very definitely back again. They may be disguised as drapery. Augustabernard does this by using the material widthways instead of lengthways for a straight skirt and gathering it at the back in folds. And there are one or two " fish-tails."

ON the princess coat on the left a narrow fur stole is used as a collar, tied in a bow with ends hanging to the hem. The jacket of the suit on the right has sleeves of flat fur.

OVERHAULING YOUR WARDROBE

Even Tailored Suits are Bargains Now

By Odette

NOW is the time to take thorough stock of your wardrobe, and to fill all those gaps in it while the sales are on and prices are low. Of course, there are some women who refuse to shop at sale-time, saying that they cannot get what they want.

For instance, I have often been told by women who like plain, well-cut tailor-mades that such garments are not reduced in price.

If this was ever the case, it certainly is not true now. At the present moment one can see beautifully tailored suits and blouses at almost half the usual prices, while really exclusive accessories such as scarves, ties, and belts in attractive designs are available at rates that before Christmas would have applied only to the cheapest makes.

Apart from the ready-made departments, it is possible to pick up lengths of tweed and cloth of superb quality that can be made up into suits, odd skirts, jackets, and waistcoats by any of the many excellent "little" tailors that now specialise in making up their customers' own material. I have drawn at the top of the sketch a tailored ensemble that could be made from remnants of good cloth and tweed.

The sketch below this shows another wardrobe "overhaul"—a way of using up a very short length of very good material to excellent effect. Five-eighths of a yard of 36in. or 39in. material would be enough to face the brim of a hat and line a scarf of this kind. Below this again is an entirely new design for the woman who has hitherto found ermine velvet too expensive. The fronts cross over and tie in a knot at the back of the neck. One yard of 48in. fur fabric or ermine velvet will make this wrap.

Women who do not like cutting out or fitting will be glad to know that one of the most popular wraps of a leading Paris house is a straight length of black or grey ermine velvet (40in. long by 22in. wide) lined with the same ermine velvet in white. The lowest sketch shows how gracefully this can be worn for day or evening occasions.

Finally, I have given you an idea of how to renovate an old dress by introducing new sleeves, collar, and belt of completely different material. If the sleeves are sufficiently important-looking, the dress will take on quite a new look.

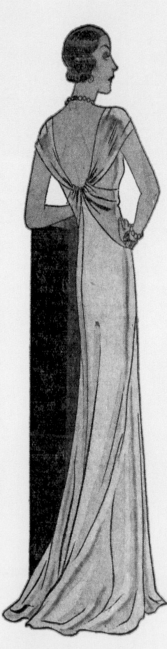

SMART WOMEN are WEARING in PARIS

Brief Capes   Longer Skirts
All-Plaid Accessories

By DARIER

HUNDREDS upon hundreds of styles, many of them conflicting, have been shown at the dress collections. Out of these a certain definite few will survive and become the modes of the season. And why? Just because women like them, buy them, and wear them!

So if you want to be in the vanguard of fashion, watch the smart women. I've been watching the smartest women in Paris, and in this article I propose to report to you the leading modes they are sponsoring.

Where All Agree

Already they have adopted enthusiastically for street wear the woollen coat-dress or frock with shallow detachable cape. Every dressmaking house reports an unprecedented demand for models of this type, and, working in almost uncanny unison, every collection shows a vast choice in just this sort of costume.

An interesting version of this style is the contrasting cape, for which a brilliant colour in thin woollen fabric, such as scarlet or bright green, is used with a flat purse made of the same material. The vivid cape and purse complete a black or dark-coloured woollen frock. I have seen several cape-boleros with flaring elbow-length sleeves worn with tailored wool or silk frocks.

For present southern wear and for later on in town, women are choosing little printed crêpe capes with deep backs that merge into long sash ends to tie about the waist. These are worn over one-toned frocks. Great favour is shown, too, for printed crêpe frocks for afternoon wear with short woollen capes in one tone matching the predominating colour of the print. These are lined with the dress print, and frequently are bordered with fox. Some little wool frocks have snugly fitting short capes.

Skirts are being worn longer for daytime. And formal evening models are so long that they settle on the floor all round and very often trail at the back. A charming dress of this type in lustrous white satin is sketched at the top left. It was worn at a recent dinner dance at a leading restaurant.

For formal afternoon wear, skirts that just cover the ankle permit a gradual transition from the shorter tailored frock to the trailing evening gown.

A Worth model in this manner has just been selected by Lady Weymouth. It is of black ciré satin, with long close sleeves topped by shallow puffs of open work done by using flattened tubing made of the satin and working it into a lacy design. The high draped neckline is gathered into a strass clip on the shoulder, and the crushed belt has strass buckles at the side.

To return to street clothes. Suit and ensemble coats are being worn in a variety of styles. The little belted jacket and the barely hip-length, slightly fitted, coatee are the favourites for suits.

Miss Gloria Swanson, who has just sailed for Hollywood, was seen in Paris in a very smart suit of dark blue wool with a white hair-line. The jacket was very short, just atop the hips, and had a wide shoulder line accentuated by "shoulder-trays" and set-in sleeves pleated at the top. With it she wore a white blouse with cowl neckline, and a dark blue knitted wool cap.

WEAR THIS— *If You're SLIM*

By Odette

A NEW type of dress, which enhances the grace of a figure with a slender waist, has had considerable success since it was launched a few weeks ago.

* * *

My sketch shows a very good example of this style. The very wide waistband is cut on the bias, and moulds the figure closely from about 2 inches above to at least 3½ inches below the normal line.

This belt is inserted into the dress to avoid any unnecessary bulk. The top part blouses slightly over this band and the skirt fits easily round the hips.

* * *

Dart tucks—combining utility with decorative

effect—trim the lower part of the blouse and sleeves and the top of the skirt.

The dress fastens in two places — about 6 inches at the back of the neck and at the side of the waistband in front. Short "plaquet holes" extend above and below the band to allow the dress to be easily slipped on and off. Through these holes can be seen a foundation of a contrasting colour.

* * *

This particular model is intended to be in pearl beige silk marocain, and is worn under a Persian lamb cloak lined with the same silk. The large muff trimmed with silver fox to match the cloak is one of the season's modes.

TO-DAY'S PAPER PATTERN

Design by Odette

FIVE COATS *in* ONE !

Odette

EVERYONE wants a useful light coat for early autumn days —and here is just the thing to meet the case. Designed by Odette, it is the second pattern to be offered in the already successful new *Daily Mail* Paper Pattern Service. Full particulars for obtaining it are given in the opposite page. The price is sixpence, post free.

The coat has the new sleeves set into deep square armholes, and a long scarf collar which can be tied in many different ways. It can be worn hanging loosely from the shoulders, or belted: and you can make it full or three-quarter length.

Five different ways of making up this pattern are shown in Odette's sketch. First on the left is a black satin coat with white crêpe sleeves to match the dress worn with it. (Black and white is the vogue in Paris.) Next you see it in brown tweed lined with

the same material as the jumper. Or you can make an unlined coat longer than the pattern in pink linen to be worn over a black crêpe or satin dress, as shown on the third figure.

Fourth comes a white homespun coat trimmed with machine stitching.

Two coats are even smarter than one this season. In the right-hand picture they are made quite separately—one of red flannel and one of heavy crash—and put on as one coat with both scarves tied together. A good idea for adapting a summer coat to autumn days.

NEWS FROM THE LONDON DRESS SHOWS

A VELVET hat, cleverly hand worked, with a matching scarf is a new Condor "set."

The Hood Cape Arrives
Two-Occasion Frocks

By Victoria Chappelle

FASHION has suddenly become less of an autocrat and more of a fairy godmother. If we feel a qualm when we watch willowy mannequins parading in the slimmest of frocks—apparently about half a yard wide at the hem—it is dispelled as we realise the enormous variety of the ideas planned for the new season. The older woman has not been made such a fuss of for years; all kinds of deficiencies in the figure can be hidden, and the plainest gowns may be made exciting with well-thought-out details.

* * *

MOST of us will still have to concentrate on diet, but just in case our will-power is not strong the designers have been thinking out clothes which will help us. One result is the dark skirt and the lighter jacket—an alliance which is worth about a week's fasting. Another is the cape, and a third an adaptation of the swagger coat—not quite so swagger this autumn but still remarkably helpful.

*

THE new plaid blouses, worn with very plain suits in a light shade or in a colour which repeats the ground of the plaid, will appeal to many women. These were very prominent at a very smart London dress show last week, with plaid jacket linings and gloves to match. Matching gloves are still an important item in the fashions shown in London salons, although they are by no means seen so much outside.

* * *

ONE of the newcomers which are eager to make themselves popular is the suit with the jacket cut like a blouse. It has been nicknamed the 11 to 7 suit, because it can be worn from morning to evening. Then there is the little shoulder cape which looks a trifle top-heavy because it is pulled back in a kind of hood. The wrap-over skirt which fastens at the back with three or four clips—guaranteed to stand any amount of pull—is another.

* * *

IF your bank balance simply will not run to fur this season, make the best of it with a scarf. Worn with a suit, it might match your blouse, and with a wool frock a cashmere scarf in a contrasting shade can be pulled through a

couple of slots cut in front. The hanging ends might be fringed, if you like that kind of thing.

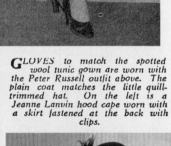

GLOVES to match the spotted wool tunic gown are worn with the Peter Russell outfit above. The plain coat matches the little quill-trimmed hat. On the left is a Jeanne Lanvin hood cape worn with a skirt fastened at the back with clips.

FRIVOLOUS FROCKS

for
Christmas

By
VICTORIA CHAPPELLE

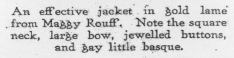

An effective jacket in gold lamé from Maggy Rouff. Note the square neck, large bow, jewelled buttons, and gay little basque.

THERE is just time now, before Christmas parties begin, to look at our frocks, make necessary alterations and adjustments, and decide what will be the smartest little indoor wrap to wear.

Something a little romantic seems to fit in to a Christmas background—frills and ruffles and those new coronets which look so well on a shining head. I have given you two suggestions in this page for a party frock.

The black net gown, as you see it, is the kind of thing for a party which is guaranteed not to be too riotous. But the gown next to it has the simple lines to which no damage can be done. And notice the "boa" of ostrich feather which is carried across the front.

IT looks like being very chilly this Christmas, so do not hesitate, if you feel the cold, to wear a frock with long sleeves.

You will be as smart as your neighbour in her backless gown, so long as you remember that a glimpse of your shoulders must be shown even if your arms are not, and that a fairly low back décolletage is necessary.

And here is another idea for the older woman who dislikes going out in the evening because she feels that her gown is not warm enough.

Wear a sleeved jacket with it, made on the newest lines — you will see an example in this page—and interline the sleeves and back with domette, that wafer-thin woollen which is one of the warmest materials imaginable.

For a Girl

I FIND nowadays that the average girl who is looking forward to wearing her first evening dress likes something dignified. Her mother got excited about filmy chiffons and tulle, but *she* prefers a thick satin, moiré, or even velvet.

Still, her dress should not be elaborate, so here is a suggestion which may be helpful. Have the dress made on princess lines, fitting snugly to the figure but not shelving in at the back, with just enough fullness given to the skirt to enable her to dance with comfort.

The neckline in front should be straight from shoulder to shoulder. At the back it may be cut in a modified cowl, or in an oval, or have a couple of wide straps criss-crossed. But the only decoration would be in the little wing sleeves, which should be piped with thick padding, row over row. The effect above rounded young arms is charming.

If white is worn, coloured accessories look well. The gloves should be bought first, in velvet, moiré, satin, or suède, and white shoes dyed to match. This is not expensive. If pos-

A "boa" of dark brown ostrich feathers crossing the corsage of the pale gold velvet Chanel gown shown above makes an unusual trimming.

On the left is a débutante gown in filmy black net with ruchings on the spreading skirt and charming little sleeves. The high front neck-line accentuates the jewelled neck and back straps.

sible, some material to match the gloves in colour and texture should be bought for a pochette. Otherwise, a white one can be carried. This kind of "set" would make rather a good Christmas present.

WE are seeing many low décolletages this season. But if you dislike them and are thinking of having a frock made for Christmas, why not follow the example of a woman I saw the other day who had had a couple of long oblong slits cut in the back of her frock on each side of her spine?

"Glove sleeves" would look attractive, too. These are merely long sleeves which stop about five inches below the shoulder and are kept up by means of elastic gussets, which can be hidden beneath a kind of cuff. These, however, do look a little elaborate, so unless your frock is perfectly plain, do not think of them. But this suggestion would help to solve the problem of the woman with too thin arms.

HATS that Change Your Character

By Victoria Chappelle

A BRIGHT touch of colour on a dark sports hat makes all the difference to your outfit. Here is a brimmed hat in rough felt, tilted at a smart angle, and with a folded crown, giving a pointed effect, finished by white and orange tassels.

TIE up your draped cap as though it were a parcel this autumn. Above is a green fancy woollen "glengarry" folded round with satin ribbon in the newest way.

THIS formal Le Monnier afternoon hat of felt and taupé carries out the same idea. The cuff brim of taupé broadens at the back round the felt crown, and the straps across the top are caught in a clip.

OUR hat-boxes, far more than our beauty boxes, will contain all we need for several changes of character this season.

* * *

THE first "buy," of course, is a beret. For morning it is big and floppy and severely plain; for afternoon it is just as big, but kept in its place, more often than not, by means of stiffening. Add a few ostrich feather tips and nothing more formal could be found.

* * *

FOR those who can stand a rather hard line, or for the days when we are at the top of our form, there are the new little caps made somewhat on the lines of a glengarry but tied up on top, rather like a parcel, with a ribbon or a band of the material. This is for the more sophisticated woman, so if you are very *ingenue*, it is best to avoid it.

* * *

THEN, of course, there are the brimmed hats which all of us need for those days when, for some reason or another, nothing goes right. They have just enough brim to give us back our self-confidence, but it must be subtly curved if the cure is to be complete.

* * *

FOR those days when you feel tailored and energetic there are felt sports hats, or the new stiffly brimmed sailors in felt or hatter's plush.

* * *

VELVET, of course, is *the* material this year—luckily for all of us. There is no other so softening, so easy to match or to blend with.

Feathers in any shape or form are at the top of their class for trimmings. Tuck them away at the back or on the top of the crown if they are fluffy, lay them on the crown if they are flat, or let them sweep over your eyebrows if your looks will stand it.

with an eye to CHRISTMAS

RINGS in pink, green, and amber unbreakable crystal, packed in a little glass box. All ready for Christmas morning!

* * *

Powder bowl in the new flat shape, and scent or lotion bottle in "smoky" glass to match.

* * *

Hats for a "cruising Christmas" in fine panama, and an attractive beret for the same purpose in white leather.

* * *

A cocktail set—tiny hat, necklace, and bracelet, all made in twisted strands of gold thread.

* * *

Mulberry kid gloves with gauntlets of plaited strips of felt in mulberry and beige; can be had in nigger and beige.

* * *

Necklace of wooden beads in dull red, green, and natural, tied at the back with narrow ends of suède, together with wooden stud earrings and a two-headed beret pin. This makes an unusual set, and will go well with a suit of "country gentlewoman's" tweeds.

* * *

Long pearl necklace with huge jade and diamanté motif.

* * *

Jumper hand-knitted in burnt orange. Has a long scarf that can be draped and folded in many ways, and polished wood buttons

* * *

Veils are important again. With their help we can face the "off the brow" hats. The newest ones are short and very stiff.

Gold or silver kid mules hand-painted in tiny floral design—a charming Christmas present.

* * *

Transparent bracelets in shades of orchid and pink—lovely with the fashionable silver lamé.

* * *

After the wine shades—ruby. Necklace, bracelet, rings and

*H*ERE *are two headdresses seen in the shops—one a simple silver band, the other a little wreath of shell flowers.*

Our Shop Detective

....

Has

....

Seen...

....

earrings are all to be had in this warm clear colour, cleverly set with diamanté.

* * *

Large envelope-shaped pochette in mulberry tweed with chromium fastening.

* * *

Bracelets of leather on steel—very effective in white.

* * *

Hat in nigger satin, with square crown and stitched peak brim, to be worn off the face and slightly tilted to the right. This is an advance model and gives some idea of what we may expect in the spring.

* * *

Apple green crêpe evening bag finely embroidered in diamanté. Also an oval bag in black antelope, fastened by a big jade button.

* * *

The smallest portable gramophone—folds up like a camera and has a green lacquer finish.

* * *

Feather flowers for decora-

*T*HESE *elegant evening gloves, more like pull-on sleeves than the usual shaped mittens, are very effective in black chiffon—a shop "snapshot."*

tion—amusing and gay in most unnatural shapes and colours!

* * *

Bag and scarf in Scotch tweed —a present for the "country cousin."

* * *

Lamp and shade cleverly painted in boxing scenes—for a man's room.

SMART TRIMMINGS

MONKEY fur is back again in the guise of ingenious trimmings. Since black with white, black with grey, or black with string colour are three of the season's smartest alliances, this light and glossy fur lends itself to admirable effects.

The upper sketch on the right shows an elbow-length cape of monkey fur tied at the shoulder with a lacquered satin ribbon. A wide "bow" of the fur. matching the fringe of fur on the gauntlet gloves of black antelope, is worn by her companion.

THE possibilities of white organdi for evening have not yet been exhausted, and one of the most charming summer accessories is the organdi boa which can be worn over practically any type of gown. On the left you see a pale yellow boa cut in chrysanthemum petals closely massed.

A boa in one circular piece which is slipped over the head and draped carelessly over the shoulders is shown in the lower sketch. It is composed entirely of circular ruffles cut from white organdi.

MY PARIS DRESS SHOW
NOTEBOOK

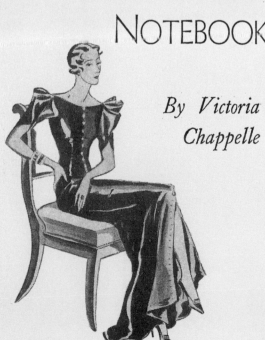

By Victoria Chappelle

ONE is forcibly reminded of mid-Victorian upholstery —as seen in portraits of the period—when looking at some of the materials in the present dress collections.

The striped velvets — sometimes in two colours—and the satins which are being used for some of the new frocks and jumpers might have been copied from those rather dreary fabrics. They are not particularly becoming — but Paris obviously thinks them worth while !

SQUARE shoulders will share their importance next season with small square cape-collars. These are running through the collections like an epidemic. Whether in material and edged with fur, or in a flat fur-like astrakhan, the principle is nearly always much the same—the collar is drawn up close to the neck and then fluted over the shoulders and along the back and the front. The same idea is achieved with a long strip of fox fur occasionally.

IT is interesting to note how many designers have determined to do without lavish fur this year. In consequence, some of the less formal coats have a good deal more interest about the neckline. Elizabethan ruffles in the coat material, padded rolls, rows of piping, or scarves made of plaided strips of the material are among the intelligent efforts made to solve the problem.

Glove interest has waned considerably. It is true that one house uses three-quarter sleeves with long fur-gauntleted gloves, but this is an isolated case. Gloves of green tweed to match a coat and frock, which,

AN EGG MASK FOR BEAUTY

TREATMENT YOU CAN DO AT HOME

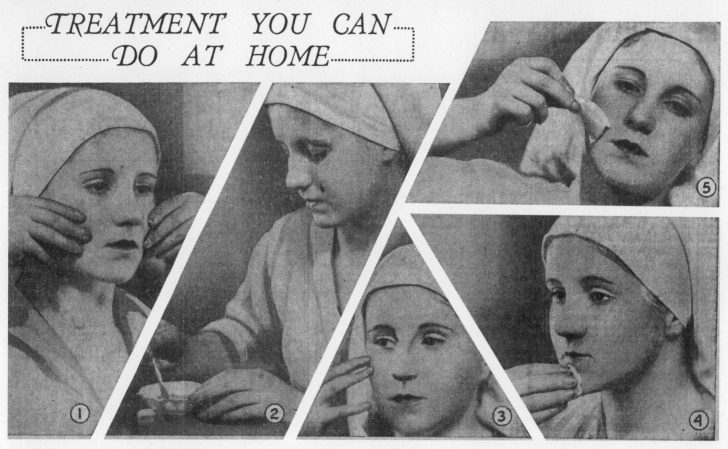

SUPPLEMENT the good work of your cleansing and nourishing creams by giving your face an occasional egg mask. It will strengthen the muscles and greatly improve the texture of the skin.

1. *Remove all dust and make-up with cleansing cream. Wipe off thoroughly. Pat muscle oil round the corners of nose and mouth. Wipe off.*

2. *Separate the yolk from the white of one egg. Put white* aside *and beat the yolk. You will not require the white.*

3. *Spread the beaten yolk quickly and evenly over face and neck with finger tips. Leave to dry in a crust. This should take only a few minutes.*

4. *Remove egg yolk with cotton wool soaked in cold rose-water.*

5. *Pat the face smartly with a pad soaked in astringent before making up as usual.*

Look Lovely To-day!

A LOTION made of one part white wine vinegar to three parts distilled water will remove that light crop of freckles after a day at the seaside.

Protect Your Eyes

If you are spending a day on the beach, beware the glare of the sea. Take either a brimmed hat, sun-glasses or an eye-shade. The latter are smart in piqué with a green lining, and can be had with or without a net to keep the hair in place. Bathe the eyes when you get home at night in warm water with a pinch of boric powder added.

For the Nose

This prominent member is the first to receive the sun's attention. Even if you let your complexion "go" for the day's outing, treat your nose with vanishing cream or cream with a powder base. This is available in all smart flesh shades.

An Evening Cocktail

If you have remembered to bring your tube of liquefying cleansing cream, your handbag flask of eau-de-Cologne or astringent, your rouge compact and powder, you can give yourself a facial "cocktail" in five minutes at the end of the day and emerge fresh and fragrant for the evening's amusement.　　　　　*J. B.*

Have You a Film Face?

By a Cinema Director

CYNICS say that the perfect film face is made in the studio beauty parlour!

There is plenty of truth in this gibe, for miracles are wrought in our beauty shop. But there is a naturally perfect film face, and when a girl of this rare type walks under the lights for the first time an expert can spot her immediately.

She has a pale skin of fine texture which needs the minimum of make-up. Her hair is auburn—*not* platinum blonde—and has wonderfully effective lights and shadows. Her eyes are dark and sparkling, set rather wide apart, and her brow is low and broad. White, perfectly even teeth are almost essential. But the shape of the mouth does not matter very much, provided it is not ultra wide, for new mouths can very easily be sketched in with lipstick. A delicate nose, no matter whether *retroussé* or Roman, a clear profile, long neck and well-poised head complete my perfect film beauty.

Wide-set eyes and a dazzling smile—Miss Loretta Young, a classic beauty of the films.

Contradictory

Now someone will mention at least a dozen stars in the first rank who are entirely unlike that. I admit that there are many, but each one has some quality, apart from facial beauty, which has made it worth while to spend on her our skill in make-up and lighting. Each has an expressive face which clearly mirrors the personality of the actress. That is almost the only quality which cannot be faked for the screen.

Make your Bathroom your Beauty Parlour

THIS dressing-table is built for the bathroom beauty parlour. In sea-green cellulose, it has a special mirror with damp-proof backing.

THE fastidious woman, whenever circumstance allows, will find it a great joy to have her beauty "work-table" in her bathroom, keeping on her bedroom toilet table merely her perfume spray and decorative brushes and comb. If she is living, after the modern fashion, in a one-room-and-bath flatlet, she can dispense with a dressing-table altogether in the bed-sitting-room.

Labour Saving

Nearly always the light in the bathroom is good, water is at hand, and there is no risk of spoiling carpets or dainty covers with powder and spilled lotions.

If it is not practicable to keep one's beauty things in the bathroom, it is a good idea to have a fitted-up bag, that can be carried from bedroom to bathroom, to contain all that is necessary to facial grooming.

Toilet bags with lightning fasteners are shaped like ordinary handbags, and contain face towel, tissues, two pots for cleansing and massage creams, and two bottles for lotions.

For Travelling

Baths, basins, towels, toothbrushes, and face gloves have long since "gone gay," and now sponges can be had in orchid-mauve, buttercup-yellow, powder-blue, and flesh-pink.

Newcomers are capsules of pine needle salts (break one into your bath and you will imagine you are lying in a pine forest on a summer's day!); a romantic bath essence with dusting powder to match; cottonwool containers in pastel enamels, or a grander chromium affair for face tissues, meant to fix on the wall.

Or what about soap, shaped like a pineapple, which divides into sections and is perfumed with orange and citron? Or a telescopic back puff which packs into a small box, and is indispensable in these days of the backless gown?

Any of these things might well be an essential part of the modern woman's bathroom equipment all the year round.

Lifestyle

When not cooking, dressing, putting on makeup, doing household tasks or holding down a job, how did women in the 1930s enjoy themselves? Here again, the Daily Mail was on hand to guide them. How to give a dinner party without a cook? Simple. Rather than look harassed and make her guests uncomfortable, choose a fool-proof menu which can be prepared well in advance, even if it is something basic like Irish stew and fruit salad. ("It doesn't matter if you're little maid-of-all-work *does* make a mistake and hand from the right side now and again," writes the author). How to dance a tango in the night-club? Here are all 10 movements of the Right-hand Promenade Turn. Thin-faced? A touch of rouge on the chin will make a long face look shorter. Throughout these pages, despite the growing independence of women, it is taken for granted that the woman's role is to find a husband and then to please him, by preparing his meals, doing the housework and looking radiant when he comes home. In an article called Sweeping and Dusting Your Way to Beauty, a busy housewife complains that she has no time for slimming exercises. "But the very tasks of which they complain can, if done rhythmically and with the correct poise of the body, maintain just that slimness and grace which every woman desires," explains the author triumphantly. "Housework exercises are now taught in a London school where women learn rhythm in everyday tasks!". The Modern Age may have dawned in the 1930s, but it still had a very long way to go.

WEEK-END OUTFIT
You Can PACK in a SUITCASE.

Week-end party invitations, now that Spring is well on the way, are beginning to pour in. Here Odette has planned an outfit which can be adapted for brief visits to country cottages or flying expeditions to Paris.

A WEEK END outfit varies according to the kind of week-end involved.

There is the week-end for which one feels one has been invited purely and simply to weed the garden, and there is the week-end during which one is rushed round to all the excitements—urban and rural—within a sixty-miles radius. There is also the week-end trip to Paris. The latter two are likely to be something of a strain on a suitcase wardrobe unless the greatest discrimination is used in the choice of garments.

Ubiquitous "Four Piece."

The new interpretation of the four-piece ensemble—a top coat, jacket, skirt and blouse—furnishes the basis of the outfit in either case. The first three items may match exactly or be of different materials that "compose" successfully.

For the ordinary week-end in a country house I would suggest a tweed top coat in a mixture of colouring that gives a pastel effect, a checked skirt that shows up the same colours more definitely, and a cardigan coat—of the new type, with four pockets and a belt, as shown at the extreme left of the sketch—of either flannel or suède tricot in one of the brighter colours of the tweed.

This cardigan may be plain, or bordered with narrow bands of the skirt material as shown in the sketch. A silk shirt worn with a tie or large bow, a felt hat in a pastel shade to match the overcoat, loose chamois gloves, and brown calf shoes, with thick silk or cashmere stockings, complete the ensemble.

What to Pack.

All these things will be worn for the journey, whether by road or rail, leaving the suitcase accommodation free for underclothing and night attire, a spare shirt or thin woollen jumper, a simple crêpe day dress, an evening dress of printed chiffon or lace that can be packed into a small space without showing creases, heavy shoes for golf or walking, satin shoes for the evening, a beret or tricot cap, and a compact array of toilet requisites.

It is taken for granted that underclothing of the most modern type is chosen—silk tricot combinations with woven brassière tops, instead of yesterday's cami-knickers, tailored knickers that dispense with every vestige of superfluous fullness, and an unlined dressing-gown of printed silk and on severely masculine lines.

In the Sketch.

The sketch shows two excellent top coats (on the 2nd and 4th figures from the left). Both have loose armholes that enable them to be worn over another jacket quite comfortably. The latter has the short scarf collar that is having a great success in Paris, and is trimmed with lines of stitching; the former has the fullness at the waistline disposed of by tucks and an *inserted* belt.

On this figure is shown, too, one of the most effective of the new tweed and felt hats for motoring. The tweed "brim" is continued at either side into long scarf ends which are crossed in front and carried round to the back of the neck, where they are tied or knotted

"Transformation" Tie.

Many of the new coats are made without collars of any kind, but are supplied with separate cravat ties. The figure at the extreme right shows an outfit that would form the mainstay of a similar wardrobe intended for Paris.

A dark bluish tweed is chosen for the costume and beige washing satin for the tunic. A beige felt hat and beige gloves are important items of the ensemble. Two cravat ties, one in the tweed and one in beige satin, should be included in this wardrobe. The tweed one could be worn with a tuck-in shirt and blue felt hat for travelling and morning wear, the satin one with the matching tunic for afternoons.

Accessories That Are Chic.

Among the chic accessories to the week-end outfit shown in the sketch are a tweed bag with a deep mount of inlaid wood in different colours to match those appearing in the tweed, a large bunch of field flowers, and a string of carved wooden beads. *ODETTE.*

Lady Campbell writes
Sir Malcolm's Article—and Declares
Women Drivers are Better than Men!

It is time justice was handed to the mere woman who drives her own car—Lady Campbell at the wheel.

S IR Malcolm Campbell, the Motoring Editor of "The Daily Mail," is on his way home from Miami, Florida, where last week he set up a new world's land speed record so Lady Campbell takes his place with a racy defence of the woman motorist.

This article is the first of a short series which Lady Campbell will contribute to "The Daily Mail."

◆◆◆◆◆◆◆◆◆◆◆◆◆◆◆◆◆◆◆◆◆◆◆◆◆◆

A S a regular reader of motoring articles, I have been forced to the conclusion that we women are not popular among the opposite sex, at least as drivers of motor-cars.

We Drive Better

Really it is time a little justice was handed out to the mere woman who has the audacity to insist upon driving her own car—and, on the average, does it better. Yes, Mr. Man, women *are* better drivers than men.

Let us examine the alleged offences to which we women are said to be prone.

To begin with, we know nothing about the amenities of the road and are utterly lacking in "road sense."

Fewer Accidents

If that means a knowledge of road usage which enables us to drive without being a menace to others and to keep clear of accident, then I say we do possess it, and in ever greater measure than does the male driver. Proportionately to numbers, we women drivers figure better in the accident statistics than do men.

Another charge levelled against us is that we have no mechanical sense and are rough on our cars. Once again I join issue with the attackers.

In these days of comparative mechanical perfection of the car, when every operation, including that of gear changing, has ceased to be a matter of brute force, the lighter, defter touch of the woman gives her an advantage just where she is said to be lacking.

The Gear-Crashers

Where the woman driver does score is that she is subconsciously aware of her shortcomings in this direction and therefore refrains from taking chances which the man, conscious of his superior judgment, will accept—and often find out that he is wrong.

Again, we are said to know nothing about the mechanical side of our cars. We have not, generally speaking, the remotest idea of what it is that makes the wheels go round.

I am not going to contend that every woman motorist is an accomplished mechanic, for I do know that quite a number of very competent drivers are abysmally ignorant of everything that concerns the mechanics of the motor-car, but is not the same true of men? Of course it is; and again taking the average, I am perfectly certain that we women do not lag behind our menfolk in our mechanical knowledge of the car.

There is a little something the men forget when they accuse us of this want of knowledge. I suppose I ought not to give away my sex, but the opportunity is too tempting.

I believe the West African natives will tell you that the monkey is a very clever little person. He could talk if he wanted, but he knows that, if he did, man would at once put him to work—so he doesn't !

And, speaking now as Mrs. Everywoman, I certainly am not going to jack up my own car on a muddy road to change a wheel, or to do a dirty job under the bonnet, when I can by an assumption of helpless ignorance get it done for me by a large, hefty man who is simply bubbling over with superiority.

It Saves Trouble

Then there is the question of whether women should take part in motor racing or not.

Women have proved that they are quite as capable of driving racing cars at high speed as men. The most important race at Brooklands during the year just past was won by two women driving as a team.

Just Jealousy !

I suspect that the opposition is simply due to jealousy. In the days when racing was confined to the male animal, he who drove fast cars was an idol, adored by the whole flapper tribe. Once, however, woman invaded his sphere and showed that she could more than hold her own, much of the glamour disappeared and the motor-racing male ceased to be a hero to his gallery.

Naturally he simply hated it. Hence his efforts to keep us out.

I have no wish to race again, but I am all on the side of the woman who does, because I know that on the track, as on the road, the woman driver is equal to, if not better than, the man.

WOMAN at the WHEEL

We Like Pretty Cars—but they must be Practical

By Lady (Malcolm) Campbell

WHETHER it is that I failed to find the winner of the Derby, or that none of my Irish Sweep tickets drew even a modest £100 I do not know, but I am certainly full of complaints this week.

I have been reading through the R.A.C. regulations for the conduct of Concours d'Elegance. Of course, one has to agree that these events do not entirely appeal to the woman competitor. Their clear intention is to assist in improving the breed of the motor-car, with particular attention paid to the coach-work part of the vehicle. That is excellent: but I cannot help thinking that if the R.A.C. and the trade bodies which consult with the club on these matters had asked two or three practical women motorists for their assistance the rules might have been slightly different.

* * *

MY main objection is that far too many marks are allotted for "beauty." I confess it is a joy to me to regard a beautiful motor-car, but it is a case in which beauty can be said to be only skin deep!

* * *

THERE are such considerations as comfort, convenience, ease of control, visibility of the road from the driving seat, lightness of steering,

This Schiaparelli suit of rough brown linen has a belt-purse which is useful for the woman driver.

and a dozen other points which are of the first importance to the woman who drives and looks after her own car.

I know a car—it must be nameless: it is not the only offender—which would take first prize in any competition judged on beauty of line only.

The model I mean is known as a close-coupled coupé and is as pretty as a picture. It is of the two-door type, and the doors, which are very wide, open rearwards. They are heavy, as these wide doors must be, and, if you happen to stop on a road which has a sideways slope and you want to open the door against it the physical effort needed is quite considerable.

* * *

I HAVE known doors, too, to fly open while driving. If it should happen in this case you are lucky indeed if the only damage is a pair of badly wrenched hinges. I admit that the two-door saloon, or close coupé, has its merits, but in competition I should deduct marks for such doors.

* * *

THIS same car has the change-speed lever so placed that you have to reach for it at the risk of braining yourself against the dash. You can, I believe, buy as an extra a "remote control" arrangement to make this more accessible, but the very fact is eloquent of want of thought.

You cannot, when you are in the driving seat, see anything on the near side of the radiator cap, so low is the seat pitched for beauty of outline.

I am quite sure that these low-pitched cars are entirely responsible for what is known as kerb-shyness. You think you are driving within a few inches of the edge of the road when, in fact, you are three feet away.

* * *

DOOR-HANDLES that get caught up in your sleeve or in your driving gauntlets are another abomination—and they are so unnecessary. Doors that rattle and windows that stick in their guides and refuse to wind either up or down are another of my grumbles for a thoroughly discontented week. Do, please Mr. Motor Manufacturer, cease this quest for beauty and give more attention to the points I have noted in my opening as being even more desirable than appear-

ances to the practically minded woman of the car.

I know you have done a great deal for us and are willing to do more, but don't, I beg of you, be led away by those who tell you that all we care about are good looks in the car of our choice.

* * *

I CAME across, the other day, a neat little accessory for the woman motorist who enjoys a cigarette at the wheel. This is a natty leather cigarette case, with a compartment to hold matches, which clips on the steering wheel so that one's attention is not distracted while fumbling for cigarettes and matches in the bad old way. I confess to a liking for a smoke while driving, and I find this new case quite a boon.

Another useful item I have discovered is a belt which has a round zip-fastened purse attached to it. You know what a nuisance it is to have to search through your handbag for money to pay when filling up or anything of the kind. This way of carrying your loose change saves quite a lot of time and temper.

* * *

IF you are planning a motoring holiday, let me urge you to see that the car is in the pink of condition before you start. It is so much better to anticipate trouble and remove the possible source before you start than to have your holiday spoilt by untoward happenings for which there is no earthly excuse.

Quite probably your engine has not been decarbonised since last season. Have it done now, and the valves properly ground in. Then, the oil should be changed in engine, gear-box and back axle, and the car thoroughly greased all round.

* * *

THAT you are not likely to be using the lights much now is no reason for neglecting the battery. The starter imposes a considerable drain upon it, and in most modern cars the ignition system depends upon the battery. Make up the acid level with distilled water, clean the terminals and give them a good thick coating of vaseline.

Lady Campbell studies car comfort.

A Letter to...

HOLIDAY GIRLS

from...

THOMAS COLUMB

BANK Holiday! This day of days when thousands of oh, so modern women disport themselves by land and sea! Off you go to enjoy yourselves with never a care or thought in the world . . . and that is just what I am afraid of.

Now I, as a bachelor and an observer of that life in the raw that is so very seldom mild, intend to give you, whether you like it or not, my view of some of the things you should do, and some of the things you should avoid, to heighten the charm and increase the prestige of your astonishing sex.

Many of you, of course, will patronise one of those long, low, and incredibly fast cars, piloted by the lucky man of your choice.

Then do I beseech you to sit there demurely by his side wearing a rapturous expression, just gazing from time to time at him with an adoring look. For then he will reflect that never has he taken out a girl who has shown so much intelligence and understanding. Then is the scalp yours and the poor fish hooked.

But here my heart misgives me, for I know the way otherwise slow girls behave in fast cars.

They get all "het up." They screech and yell with laughter. They sprawl all over the machine. They clutch their driver's elbow as he is turning a peculiarly congested corner. They are, in fact a menace to the life of the populace and frighten away young men from matrimony. And you river girls! How attractive you can look as you lie with easy grace in a punt clad in a delicious white, cool-looking frock, appearing so devastatingly helpless!

But the moment you take to punting yourself, the while you utter hoarse noises as you whirl the punt round in circles, your charm is gone. You become a blot on the flowing stream.

Unforgivable!

Remember, I beseech you, that every young man who takes a pretty girl for an outing on the river is convinced he can punt.

To take the law literally into your own hands wreaks havoc with a young man's self esteem. For this he will never forgive you.

Good heavens, punts are especially put on the water for girls to look girlish and wayward in.

And sea bathing!

I recall one fine day . . . here is a very sad tale in a very sad life . . . taking out a damsel with me to the sea to bathe. She was charming . . . she was fair to behold . . . but not in her bathing dress.

She tripped down to the sea with her hair dragged back from her head, wearing a bathing suit of bright purple She looked awful. She seared my eyes She made me catch the first train home.

You really must try to look your best even in the sea. Remember that your companion wants to think of you as a mermaid and not as a floating scarecrow.

Take pains with the sea. It will repay you. Cast your bread carefully upon the waters and it will return to you in an hour or less.

Now another sad tale When I was a young flying officer training to fly in the war I prevailed on my squadron commander to allow me to take up a friend of mine for a flight.

He refused. He then looked at my friend. He consented.

All went well till we were about five hundred feet up in the air. Suddenly without any warning, for she was sitting behind me, my passenger let out an appalling yell.

"Let me out." she screamed. "Let me out!"

With this she stood up and entwined her arms round my neck bellowing like an elephant.

Aeroplanes in those days had to be treated with respect. So had their pilots. With the greatest difficulty I managed to land the machine.

Then for five minutes I told my passenger exactly what I thought of her. No wedding bells rang Should the man of your choice be an airman and such a half-wit as to consent to give you a flight, just gaze at the back of his neck and say and do nothing. Then when you land love may bloom.

Longs and Shorts

Now what of hiking, that very modern frivolity and exercise with the dreadful name? Should you desire to venture forth with some cheery companions on a walking expedition, by all means wear shorts. But only, I implore you, if you are slim and of a pleasing shape.

Should the hand of Nature have slipped when delineating your contours, do not for mercy's sake attempt such a costume.

For to the discerning masculine eye there are few sights more shattering or more romance-killing than the sight of a girl who should never wear shorts but invariably does. Which is the long and short of it.

And so I might go on For I wish you all so very well on this holiday of yours, and I should be so sorry if by any thoughtless word or deed you fell in the estimation of anyone for whom you cared

For it is the little things that count in life's holidays, which may be trite, I own, but is so terrifyingly apt on this particular Monday.

Answers to Correspondents

The Daily Mail's Women's Bureau had so many letters that Victoria Chappelle, Joan Beringer and the other experts had their work cut out to answer them. Human nature was no different 70 years ago. Young women were anxious about their complexions, mothers were anxious about their children, housewives wanted to know what to do with a tin of shrimps, or soup that had come out too salty (answer, add a few slices of raw potato and cook a bit longer). Children's diets in fact were much better than today's. Asked what to bring for school lunches, Sister Cooper SRN recommends brown bread sandwiches filled with chopped banana, or grated cheese or raw carrot, honey or egg and cress. Less healthy, in retrospect, was her advice to check children's shoe size in a high street X-ray machine - something older readers will remember. Women wrote in about sagging face muscles (wear a chin-strap) and bosom development (try deep breathing). SYZ in Chelsea, needing to bleach away a tan, is told to slice off a piece of cucumber and rub it round her neck, leave it to dry and then massage with cold cream. "My knuckles are thick. How can I get them slimmer. I am only 26," asks another woman plaintively. See a doctor: you may be rheumatic, advises Joan Beringer - "meanwhile steep the fingers in a solution of warm water and Epsom Salts." How do I prevent bed springs from creaking? asks Mrs H from Bangor. Increase the tension, comes back the answer. As if we didn't know.

"DAILY MAIL" WOMEN'S BUREAU

COOKERY—Doris B. Sheridan

RECIPE for lambs' tongues cooked in a casserole.
Herne Hill.   E. H. C.

Wash and blanch the tongues, put them into a buttered casserole with sliced mixed vegetables, mixed herbs, peppercorns, and mace, and cook over quick heat for ten minutes. Add about a pint of stock, set the lid on the casserole, and cook until tender—about two hours.

Take up the tongues, remove the skins, cut each into two portions lengthwise, and brush over with glaze. Reheat in the oven and dish on a potato purée border, pouring the strained and thickened gravy round.

My lemon marmalade set when I made it, but has now turned soft. Can I re-boil it?
Sunderland.   (Miss) S.

You evidently did not boil your marmalade sufficiently fast after the sugar was added. Without adding either sugar or water, re-boil it for a few minutes until a little of the preserve, when tested on a saucer, will set well.

Why did cream buns made from choux pastry collapse when taken from the oven, and have stodgy centres?
Gloucester.   J. D.

Because the oven was not sufficiently hot. Choux pastry requires a hot oven, and éclairs and cream buns should take about half an hour to cook.

BEAUTY—Joan Beringer

SUGGEST thorough face-cleansing treatment. I use cold water, but this makes my face sore.
Risca.   S. D. H.

The face should be washed in warm water, not cold, at night. To prevent its becoming sore, cleanse before washing with cleansing cream or almond oil. Wipe off; apply a second coating, then wash the face thoroughly, using a pure unscented soap. Massage with nourishing cream, and in the morning rinse the face with cold water softened by adding a few drops of eau de Cologne.

My hair is white, dry, and inclined to be frizzy. Would a permanent wave take out the natural wave?
Rye.   (Mrs.) S.

A permanent wave, especially in the case of white hair, would tend to increase the frizziness. The scalp should be well massaged with warm olive oil before shampooing and the hair then water-waved. A net should be worn for sleeping, and a little brilliantine brushed in when dressing the hair.

When I use white or cream powder, tiny thread veins show through and give a purple effect.
Muswell Hill.   (Mrs.) H.

As you are dark, use a tinted foundation cream and a pinky natural powder, with a cream rouge of rather a dark shade. Work this well into the skin and blend it carefully. At night a little mauve or jade powder added to the ordinary powder will detract from the high colour.

DRESS—Victoria Chappelle

SUGGEST alterations to black spring coat which seems dowdy. It is unbelted and has long revers and turned down collar worked with braid to match sleeve-ends.
Burnage.   (Mrs.) F. C. Griffiths.

Make it slightly waisted by taking in side seams a little and putting a couple of darts at back. Remove braid from collar and cuffs, afterwards pressing well. Add wide black suède, leather or stitched self-material belt, with plain, smart buckle.

I have a length of Black Watch tartan. How can I use it?
Belfast.   Wondering.

Have a frock made of it, and wear it with a full-length wool crêpe navy coat. A tartan scarf and a navy beret trimmed with a tartan tab will complete a good outfit.

Spring or summer outfit for 16-years-old girl, who looks older.
Queenborough.   Micky.

Long navy princess coat over patterned frock (navy and white or similar alliance) for summer. Grey suit with dark jumper, say blue; or navy suit with lighter blue jumper.

My hip-length suède jacket is much too narrow.
Newport.   M. E. M.

Make a waistcoat front of matching suède or thin rough woollen material in same green, fastening with buttons. If you cannot attach this to the side seams of jacket, put a couple of straps at waist to fasten at the back, with a loop at the top to pass behind your neck. The jacket can remain open or be buttoned on to the waistcoat.

What to wear with black, white, green and red herringbone tweed jacket.
Wroughton.   (Miss) J. E. Coxon.

Your own idea of a green wrap-over skirt is quite good. You can make alliance with the coat by collar, cuffs, and belt of the same green.

CHILDREN & THE NURSERY—Sister Cooper, S.R.N.

HOW to prevent a baby from turning on his face when sleeping.
Harrow.   F. L. B.

Provide a chaff pillow, and, until the habit is overcome, use webbing shoulder straps. Make sure feeding is correct, as to lie on the face sometimes indicates indigestion.

When is baby's 10 p.m. feed discontinued?
Eccles.   (Mrs.) B.

This feed is decreased at 10 months and discontinued by the first birthday, though some babies progress well on four feeds a day earlier than this.

Approximate hours of sleep required by children between 6 and 15 years.
Leamington.   Anxious.

A child of six years needs 12 hours, nine years 11 hours, twelve years 10½ hours, fifteen years 9 hours.

I have difficulty in controlling my daughter at times; she seems to need a good old-fashioned spanking!
Herts.   John Blunt.

There are two opinions on the "spanking" question. I myself feel that there are other more satisfactory ways of maintaining discipline. To smack does not encourage self-control or independence, or enable the child to act rightly when there is no one to smack her. You are representing yourself as one who inflicts pain, not one who understands the activities and interests of a child. Remember the force of example, and do not fix your standard too high for the child's age.

Directions for making a sheath for protruding ears.
Catford.   (Mrs.) E.

Choose a wide mesh net and have a band in front, passing over the top of baby's head, down over the ears, and fastening under his chin. The cap should be worn only at night.

FIVE experts are ready to solve YOUR problems! Write to-day—and remember to enclose with your inquiry form a stamped addressed envelope! Only a very small proportion of the hundreds of letters received can be printed—the rest are answered by post. Address to the "Daily Mail" Women's Bureau, Northcliffe House, London, E.C.4, marking the topic—whether cookery, beauty, children, housewifery, or dress—at the top left-hand corner of the envelope.

HOUSEHOLD HINTS ABC

from Jennifer Snow's Postbag

ALABASTER light bowls that have become yellow can be whitened if you dust very carefully, then wash in warm soapy water to which you have added an equal quantity of hydrogen peroxide. Rinse in clear warm water, and dry well. The bowl must not be allowed to stay in the water. Lay it on the table and wash by rubbing with a wet flannel.

BLACK CHARMALAINE which has become shiny can be improved by sponging with a cloth wrung tightly out of dark blue water. Rub over with a dry cloth and press on the wrong side with a moderate iron.

COCO MATTING can be cleaned, even when very dirty and stained, with hot soapy water and a dash of ammonia. Use 1 tablespoonful of ammonia to 1 quart of water.

LIME can sometimes be prevented from clogging household pipes if a fur collector—a piece of loofah—is kept in the tank and renewed from time to time.

OIL PAINTINGS which are dry and cracked should be rubbed with refined linseed oil. A very little of the oil is required at a time, and it must be completely rubbed in, otherwise the action of the air causes it to solidify which will ruin the appearance of the paintings.

SOCKS which have shrunk should be soaked in lukewarm water for 10 minutes, using 1oz. of borax to 1 gallon of water. Then wash by squeezing in lukewarm soapy water till clean. Do not rub any part of the sock. Rinse in lukewarm water, and put through the wringer till no more moisture can be extracted. Put to dry in a warm place, but not too close to fire.

WINDOW LEATHERS should be soaked, when new, for 10 minutes in lukewarm water and vinegar—⅓ gill of vinegar to 1 quart of water. Rinse in lukewarm water, squeeze in lukewarm soapy water, rinse in another soapy water, press in a cloth till no more moisture can be extracted, put to dry in a warm place, and when nearly dry pull gently on the cross and rub between the hands. On future occasions, omit the steeping in vinegar, using the soapy water treatment only.

The Week's Fashion Note

That Feathery Touch

EVERY Paris dress show features feathers in some original form. Here you see some of them.

For instance—at the top left—there is a fine straw turban with a close mass of tiny ostrich tips at the back to give that high line so fashionable just now. The collarette is composed of similiar tips arranged in two regular rows, curled in towards the centre and mounted on a satin ribbon that ties at one side.

A beret made of small iridescent breast-feathers, starting in the centre of the top, is shown in the lower sketch. The close-fitting collar, also of breast feathers, ties at the back with a bow of midnight-blue velvet ribbon.

At the right you see the unusual sleeve-trimming of a new cocktail-frock—a double row of marabout tips.

Volcanoes
& Earthquakes

A TEMPLAR BOOK
First published in the UK in 2008 by Templar Publishing,
An imprint of The Templar Company plc,
The Granary, North Street,
Dorking,
Surrey,
RH4 1DN
www.templarco.co.uk

Conceived and produced by Weldon Owen Pty Ltd
61 Victoria Street, McMahons Point
Sydney, NSW 2060, Australia

Copyright © 2008 Weldon Owen Inc.
First published 2008

Group Chief Executive Officer John Owen
President and Chief Executive Officer Terry Newell
Publisher Sheena Coupe
Creative Director Sue Burk
Concept Development John Bull, The Book Design Company
Editorial Coordinator Mike Crowton
Vice President, International Sales Stuart Laurence
Vice President, Sales and New Business Development Amy Kaneko
Vice President, Sales: Asia and Latin America Dawn Low
Administrator, International Sales Kristine Ravn

Project Editor Lachlan McLaine
Designer Helen Woodward, Flow Design & Communications

ISBN: 978-1-84011-737-0

Colour reproduction by Chroma Graphics (Overseas) Pte Ltd
Printed by SNP Leefung Printers Ltd
Printed in China 5 4 3 2 1

A WELDON OWEN PRODUCTION

► **in**siders

Volcanoes
& Earthquakes

Ken Rubin

templar publishing

Contents

in*troducing*

Under the Surface

Restless Planet   8

Spreading Seas   10

Tectonic Collisions   12

Hot Spots   14

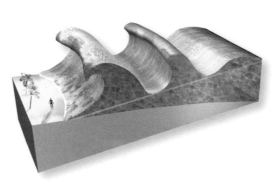

Fire Down Below

Anatomy of a Volcano   16

Types of Eruptions   18

Lava and Ash   20

Volcanic Landscapes   22

Thermal Springs and Geysers   24

Volcanologists in the Field   26

On Shaky Ground

When the Earth Moves   28

Earthquake Preparation   30

After an Earthquake   32

The Making of a Tsunami   34

Seismologists in the Field   36

in *focus*

Volcanoes

Toba   40

Vesuvius   42

Krakatau   44

Mount St Helens   46

Kilauea   48

Earthquakes

Lisbon   50

San Francisco   52

Hebgen Lake   54

Kobe   56

Indian Ocean Tsunami   58

Worlds Alive   60

Glossary   62

Index   64

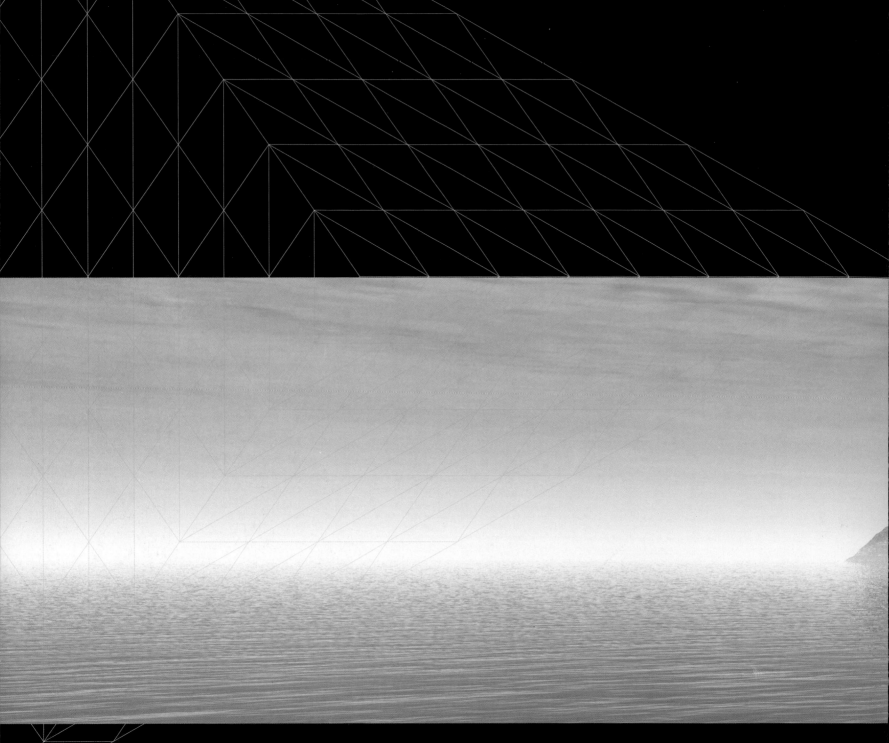

in*troducing*

Restless Planet

It might seem to us that nothing is more solid than the ground beneath our feet and that nothing is more permanent than the mountains and the oceans, but in fact our planet is restless and alive. Between Earth's thin rocky crust and its iron core lies the mantle, a zone of very hot, partially molten rock that slowly circulates. This movement pushes and pulls at gigantic slabs of the crust, which are called tectonic plates. This movement can sometimes be felt as earthquakes, and where the plates collide, or where new crust is formed, volcanoes can be found delivering hot molten rock to the surface.

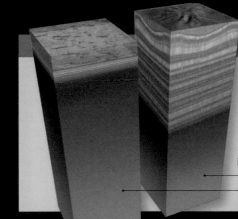

CRUST COMPARED

Earth's crust is composed chiefly of granite and basalt—two types of volcanic rock. Its thickness varies, but it is thinnest on the ocean floor, where it can be only 8 kilometres (5 mi) deep. Over the continents it is up to eight times thicker.

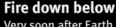

Continental crust

Oceanic crust

History of Earth
Our planet had a hot and fiery birth nearly 4.6 billion years ago. Since then, Earth has cooled and aged and become a cradle for life.

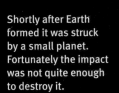

The Earth was born when some of the dust and gas circling the infant Sun came together under the force of gravity.

Shortly after Earth formed it was struck by a small planet. Fortunately the impact was not quite enough to destroy it.

The debris from this huge impact quickly assembled in Earth's orbit to form the Moon.

Gradually Earth cooled and an outer crust developed. Volcanoes and comets added water to the atmosphere and oceans formed.

Fire down below
Very soon after Earth formed it separated into layers: a dense, iron-rich core encased within a rocky mantle, surrounded by a hot gaseous atmosphere. With time a crust formed and water condensed to make great oceans. Hot material within the mantle slowly rises towards the crust while cooler material sinks. This motion is called convection.

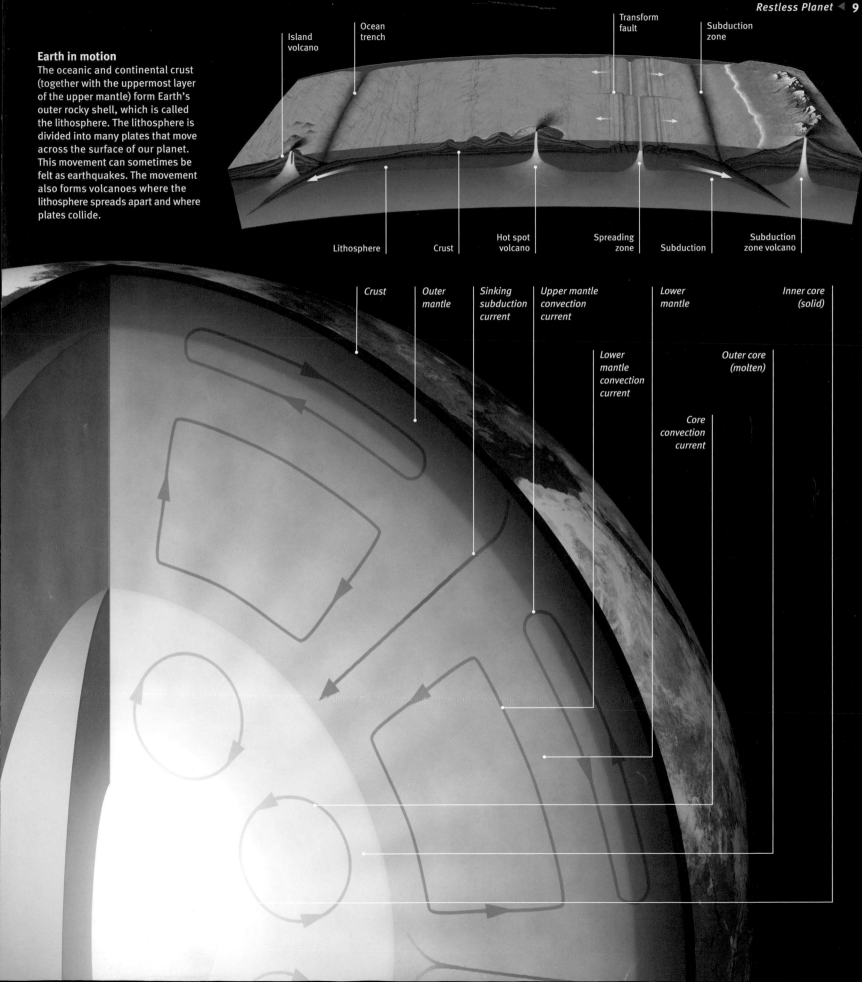

Earth in motion

The oceanic and continental crust (together with the uppermost layer of the upper mantle) form Earth's outer rocky shell, which is called the lithosphere. The lithosphere is divided into many plates that move across the surface of our planet. This movement can sometimes be felt as earthquakes. The movement also forms volcanoes where the lithosphere spreads apart and where plates collide.

Island volcano

Ocean trench

Transform fault

Subduction zone

Lithosphere

Crust

Hot spot volcano

Spreading zone

Subduction

Subduction zone volcano

Crust

Outer mantle

Sinking subduction current

Upper mantle convection current

Lower mantle

Inner core (solid)

Lower mantle convection current

Outer core (molten)

Core convection current

Spreading Seas

Deep beneath the ocean, where one tectonic plate meets another, are giant mountain ranges called mid-ocean ridges. Here, new crust is born and spreads apart. When the crust spreads quickly, the ridge is usually a broad, rounded mountain called a rise, but when the crust moves slowly, most ridges have a deep valley along their tops. No one knew the ocean ridges were there until they were discovered by surveys of the ocean floor in the 1920s. Scientists have now seen them with their own eyes and have discovered an eerie, dark world where superheated water spews from mineral chimneys as high as 15-storey buildings and strange forms of life survive.

Fire of the deep

This illustration shows a rift valley at the top of an ocean ridge. Most of the volcanic activity occurs in a narrow (1 kilometre [0.5 mi] or less) zone at the centre of the valley. Lava erupts only periodically out of fissures lining the floor while black smoker mineral chimneys can remain active for decades or even centuries.

An ocean is born

The Red Sea (seen here from space) shows where Arabia is pulling away from Africa, splitting open the continental crust. Eventually an ocean may form here, as Africa and Arabia continue to move apart and the volcanic seafloor grows wider.

Terraces *Faulting and lava flooding commonly create steps on rift valley walls.*

Mid-ocean ridge map

The mid-ocean ridge system (the blue lines on the map above) snakes its way throughout all the ocean basins. The fastest spreading ridges are in the Pacific, and the slowest are in the Arctic and south-west Indian oceans. On average the plates move apart by about 6 centimetres (2.5 in) a year.

Crust spreading

All the continents we recognise today were once joined up in a supercontinent called Pangaea. Over time Pangaea broke apart when upwelling magma split the continental crust and new oceans were born, including the Indian and Atlantic. This process is happening today in parts of eastern Africa.

Faults form when convection currents split the land. The land tilts and drops to create a wide valley between two fault scarps.

When the land drops below sea level, water floods in and fills the valley. Seafloor forms and pushes the land masses apart.

The ocean grows steadily wider as spreading continues. As the seafloor moves outward, it settles and sinks, leaving a high ridge on either side of the rift.

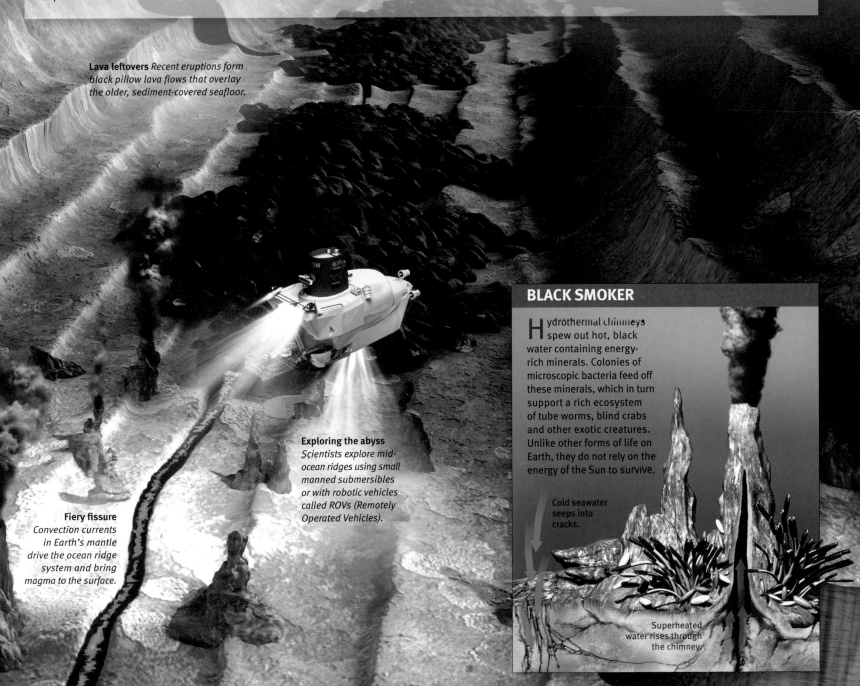

Lava leftovers *Recent eruptions form black pillow lava flows that overlay the older, sediment-covered seafloor.*

Fiery fissure
Convection currents in Earth's mantle drive the ocean ridge system and bring magma to the surface.

Exploring the abyss
Scientists explore mid-ocean ridges using small manned submersibles or with robotic vehicles called ROVs (Remotely Operated Vehicles).

BLACK SMOKER

Hydrothermal chimneys spew out hot, black water containing energy-rich minerals. Colonies of microscopic bacteria feed off these minerals, which in turn support a rich ecosystem of tube worms, blind crabs and other exotic creatures. Unlike other forms of life on Earth, they do not rely on the energy of the Sun to survive.

Cold seawater seeps into cracks.

Superheated water rises through the chimney.

Tectonic
Collisions

Earth's tallest mountains and deepest ocean trenches form where tectonic plates collide. In many places these collisions form subduction zones—places where old ocean crust is destroyed and returned to the mantle, carrying sediment and seawater with it. The immense forces of colliding plates can melt rock, forming many of Earth's most destructive volcanoes at subduction zones. Continental crust is not dense enough to return to the mantle, so where two continental plates collide, the crust is fractured, folded and thrust up. Huge mountain ranges, such as the Himalayas and Alps, are formed in this way.

Plate boundaries map
Most collision zones (highlighted in red) ring the vast Pacific Ocean or stretch from Australia to Europe along the margins of an ancient sea called Tethys.

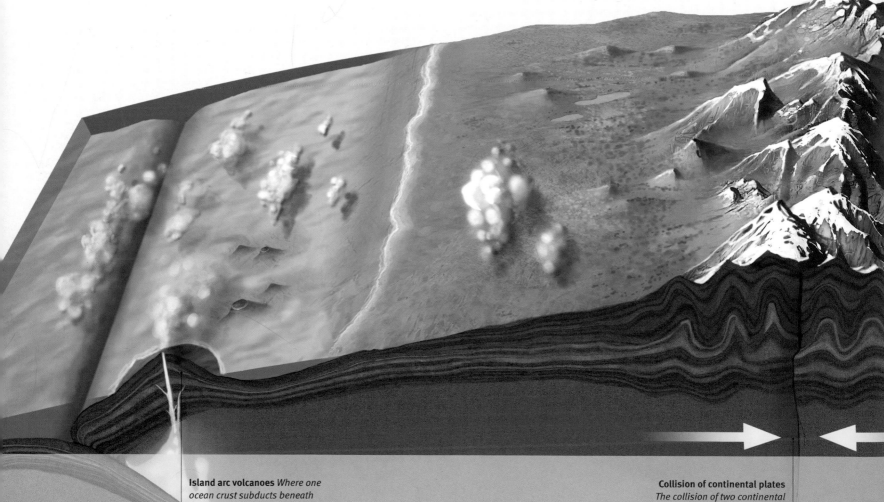

Island arc volcanoes *Where one ocean crust subducts beneath another, the subducting plate begins to melt in the underlying mantle. These are zones of intense volcanic activity and earthquakes.*

Collision of continental plates
The collision of two continental plates folds and crumples the crust into high mountain belts that can change global weather patterns and produce giant landslides.

CREATION OF THE HIMALAYAS

Earth's highest and youngest mountain range—the Himalayas—was created from a slow but mighty collision between the Indian subcontinent and Asia.

1 On the move About 200 million years ago the ancient supercontinent called Pangaea broke up, and India began to move northwards.

2 Big impact India rammed into Asia about 50 to 40 million years ago, marking the start of Himalayan uplift.

3 Mountains in motion Uplift reached full intensity 10 million years ago and continues today.

Mountains and trenches

The forces at work when tectonic plates collide are immense. No other geological process has the power to form the landscape in such dramatic ways.

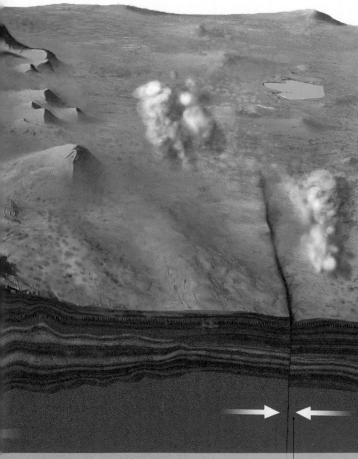

Mid-plate continental strain *Plate motions can build up enormous stresses within a single plate and cause the land to buckle or fracture.*

Coastal mountains *Continental arc volcanoes sit at the edge of a land mass, above the spot where a subducting ocean plate begins to melt in the mantle.*

Ocean trench *Deep trenches form where an oceanic plate subducts beneath another plate. The deepest places in the ocean are the trenches of the western Pacific.*

Hot Spots

Some of Earth's most magnificent volcanoes and largest outpourings of magma form above hot spots—places where a plume of hot magma pierces the lithosphere like a blowtorch. Most hot spot volcanoes occur away from the edges of Earth's tectonic plates, forming volcanoes that rise up dramatically from the neighbouring landscape. A hot spot stays still while the plate above it moves. Over millions of years this produces a line of volcanoes as the plate moves over the hot spot. Hot spot volcanoes are found above both oceanic crust (like Hawaii) and continental crust (like Yellowstone).

Hot spot Hawaii The action of a hot spot and a moving plate is apparent in this photo of the Hawaiian Islands taken from space. Magma is being fed to the large island in the lower right corner. The other islands were formed in the same place but were carried away as the Pacific plate slowly moved to the north-west.

Quiet maturity *Plate motion moves the volcano away from the magma source, and volcanism wanes. Erosion takes over and the island begins to shrink.*

First in line *The volcano closest to the hot spot gets most of the magma supply and grows rapidly.*

Birth of an island *Hot mantle rises and melts at hot spots, creating a ready supply of magma to feed volcanoes above. At oceanic hot spots volcanoes grow from the seafloor to breach the sea surface after about a million years.*

Oceanic hot spot

Volcanoes form, grow and die as they ride the lithosphere over a mantle hot spot. A single hot spot can send magma to more than one volcano at a time. The combination of a local magma source and a moving plate produces a chain of volcanoes that become progressively older in the direction of plate motion.

Hot spots map
Hot spots occur seemingly randomly all over the globe, beneath both oceans and continents. Although widely distributed, as with volcanoes, their activity levels vary dramatically. Some are dormant but are likely to reawaken in the future.

Fading away *Millions of years later, and hundreds of kilometres from the hot spot, the once great volcano barely sticks its nose above sea level, but if the ocean is warm enough, a fringing coral reef forms an atoll.*

Returned to the deep *Slowly but surely the plate slides down a subduction zone, taking its remnant hot spot volcanoes back into the mantle.*

Caldera *Infrequent, very large eruptions can drain the magma from beneath the volcano, forming a circular depression called a caldera.*

Ring fault and hills *Hills surrounding a caldera are remnants of the once great volcano that stood there and show where the caldera floor dropped along a ring-shaped fault.*

Continental hot spot

When a hot spot wells up beneath a continental plate, its progress is often slowed down by the weight of crust above it. Huge volumes of magma can accumulate between occasional massive eruptions.

The monster sleeps *A huge magma reservoir—wider than a big city—can form in the crust between eruptions.*

Highest volcanoes by continent

Although many mountains have higher summits, Hawaii's Mauna Kea is the greatest mountain on Earth. Measured from the ocean floor from which it rises, Mauna Kea towers at over 9,500 metres (31,000 ft).

Elevation (ft)

Elevation (m)

1. **Nevado Ojos del Salado, S. America**
   6,908 m (22,664 ft)
2. **Kilimanjaro, Africa**
   5,892 m (19,331 ft)
3. **Damavand, Asia**
   5,681 m (18,638 ft)
4. **Elbrus, Europe**
   5,642 m (18,510 ft)
5. **Pico de Orizaba, N. America**
   5,610 m (18,406 ft)
6. **Mt. Sidley, Antarctica**
   4,181 m (13,717 ft)
7. **Mauna Kea, Hawaii**
   4,181 m (13,717 ft) above sea level
   5,500 m (18,000 ft) below sea level

Anatomy of a
Volcano

When heat deep inside Earth melts rocks, a hot, thick liquid called magma forms. It rises and collects in large underground chambers, where small crystals begin to form, and water and gases separate out as bubbles. Under pressure from the overlying rock, the gases and fresh magma from below, the magma bursts through cracks in Earth's crust as lava or volcanic ash. Steam, gas and rock form clouds of smoke during eruptions. Fragments of rock and lava are blown out as volcanic ash and cinder. Small, hot bombs of lava shoot out of the volcano and harden in flight.

Central conduit *The main conduit rises from the magma chamber below. Magma and gases flow up the conduit to erupt through the main vent as lava or volcanic ash.*

Dyke *A vertical or near-vertical channel through which magma has pushed its way is called a dyke. The magma can break through Earth's surface to form a volcanic vent.*

Fissure eruption *Eruptions that happen from vents aligned along a crack rather than a single opening in the crust are called fissure eruptions. They can reach many kilometres in length.*

What lies beneath

Within the solid rock of a volcano there are chambers and conduits of molten magma. To determine what is inside a volcano, volcanologists study seismic data, ground deformation and minerals in the erupted lava.

Crater *Lava, ash, gas and steam erupt from this funnel-shaped opening at the top or sides of the volcano. Craters range from a few metres to many kilometres across.*

Side vent *When magma forces its way to the surface along a conduit that does not lead to the main vent, it produces a new opening that is called a side, or flanking, vent.*

Cone *The cone of the volcano is built up by ash and lava from past eruptions.*

Laccolith *Magma does not always find its way to the surface. Laccoliths are dome-shaped intrusions of magma that can push up overlying layers of rock.*

Types of volcanoes

Volcanoes are classified by the kinds of rock they are made of, by their shape and by their eruption history. Conditions at Earth's surface during eruptions, whether they involve air, water or ice, also affect the type of volcano that is formed.

Cinder cone Mildly explosive eruptions build up cone-shaped hills of volcanic cinders around a central vent. Eruptions that form cinder cones sometimes end with lava flows that can fill the crater.

Composite or stratovolcano These tall, steep-sided volcanoes are formed when multiple eruptions deposit alternating layers of volcanic ash and lava. They are widely admired for their conical shape.

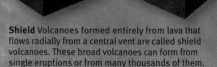

Shield Volcanoes formed entirely from lava that flows radially from a central vent are called shield volcanoes. These broad volcanoes can form from single eruptions or from many thousands of them.

Fissure and rift A linear fracture of Earth's surface through which magma has erupted forms a fissure volcano. Alternating eruptions and spreading of the rock on either side of the fissure forms a rift volcano.

VEI: 0 1 2 3 4 5 6 7 8 9

① Kilauea, Hawaii 1983–present
② Stromboli, Italy c.2000 BC–present
③ Nevado del Ruiz, Colombia 1985
④ Mt. St Helens, USA 1980
⑤ Vesuvius, Italy AD79
⑥ Pinatubo, Philippines 1991
⑦ Krakatau, Indonesia 1881
⑧ Tambora, Indonesia 1815
⑨ Taupo, New Zealand AD186
⑩ Toba, Indonesia 73,000 years ago

Volcanic Explosivity Index

The Volcanic Explosivity Index (VEI) is a scale used to categorise the size and power of eruptions. The VEI uses a logarithmic scale, meaning that an increase of one on the scale represents a tenfold increase in eruption size and power. The location and VEIs of some famous eruptions are shown on the left.

Types of Eruptions

Volcanoes erupt in many ways, emitting a combination of gases, lava and fragmented rock particles called pyroclasts. Eruptions can shoot out from a central vent or multiple vents, which are called fissures if the vents lie along a line. The type of eruption depends on many factors, such as how much magma has accumulated within the volcano, magma temperature and composition and whether or not water is present (such as in a lake or an ocean). Volcanologists recognise two main types of eruptions: effusive, when lava flows gently from the volcano; and explosive, when huge clouds of material violently shoot out from the volcano and subsequently fall to the ground.

Plinian
Named after the ancient Roman Pliny the Younger, who described the Mount Vesuvius eruption in AD79, Plinian eruptions can shoot material 45 kilometres (30 mi) high and disperse material far and wide. A special class called Ultraplinian occurs very rarely but is even more powerful.

MEASURING ERUPTIVE VOLUME

The amount of material ejected by a volcano gives a good indication of its overall power. Eruptive volumes can vary widely, from small-house-size deposits to something tens of millions times larger.

2,800 km³ (670 mi³)	100 km³ (24 mi³)	80 km³ (19 mi³)	18 km³ (4.25 mi³)	10 km³ (2.4 mi³)	3 km³ (0.7 mi³)	1 km³ (0.25 mi³)
Toba	**Taupo**	**Tambora**	**Krakatau**	**Pinatubo**	**Vesuvius**	**Mt. St Helens**
VEI: 9	VEI: 8	VEI: 8	VEI: 7	VEI: 7	VEI: 6	VEI: 5

Hawaiian
Named for the Hawaiian Islands, these eruptions mainly produce lava flows—and occasionally lava lakes—from hot, runny magma. The gas-rich early stages can produce fire fountains that reach 1 kilometre (3,000 ft) high.

Strombolian
Named for the Italian volcano Stromboli, these eruptions produce explosions of glowing rock that can reach 200 metres (600 ft) into the air before falling to the ground close to the vent.

Up in smoke
Many types of eruptions are named after the characteristics of a famous volcano. But each eruption is a little different, and any volcano can experience different eruption types during its active lifetime.

Vulcanian
Named for the Italian volcano Vulcano, these eruptions are small in volume but can shoot ash and cinders up to an altitude of 20 kilometres (15 mi),dispersing material over a greater area than Strombolian eruptions.

Peleean
Named for Mount Pelée on the island of Martinique, these eruptions are like Vulcanian or Plinian ones but also produce large, fast-moving, gravity-driven flows of hot gas, rock and ash when domes of thick lava suddenly collapse.

Surtseyan
These eruptions are named after Surtsey, an island formed in 1963 off the coast of Iceland. In Surtseyan eruptions, large quantities of shallow seawater interact with hot magma to build a cone of rock fragments. If the eruption continues long enough, the vent becomes protected from seawater and the eruptions become less violent.

Lava and Ash

No two volcanoes or eruptions are exactly alike, but what they all do is spew very hot material from one or more vents that connect their hot interiors with the surface. This material can include molten lava, gas, ash and solidified rocks called blocks and bombs. Some volcanic eruptions build up thick piles of lava or pyroclastic rock close to their vent, but others send their materials far and wide, especially when the eruption column rises high into the atmosphere. Even when they are not erupting, volcanoes can emit large quantities of gas from smaller vents known as fumaroles and superheated water from gurgling volcanic springs.

Ash distribution
Volcanic ash sometimes rises in tall plumes into the stratosphere. Here it can be swept great distances by the prevailing winds.

Lava tube breakout *Lava can flow for many kilometres through lava tubes before emerging at the surface.*

Fire curtain *Fluid lava can erupt through a line of vents (a fissure) to make a curtain of fire.*

Aa flow *This type of lava flow (pronounced "ah-ah") was named by the Hawaiians for its rough, jumbled, jagged surface.*

FORMATION OF A LAVA TUBE

Sometimes lava travels through sub-surface channels that can become tubular caves when the flow is exhausted.

❶ A river of molten lava flows in an open channel down the side of a volcano.

Hot lava flow

❷ With time the upper surface and sides of the channel begin to cool and coalesce, forcing the flow through the centre of the channel.

Lava river

❸ Eventually the entire upper surface cools to a solid crust, leaving a subterranean lava flow that can travel great distances in this insulated tube.

Hard tube

❹ When the eruption stops and the lava drains away, a hollow tunnel called a lava tube is left behind. These can be higher and wider than train tunnels.

Lava danger *Almost all lava moves slowly enough that people can escape the danger. However, trees, buildings, signs and cars will ignite when overrun by the red-hot liquid.*

Lava bomb *Chunks of once molten rock can cool and solidify as they fly through the air to become solid lava bombs that can take many distinctive aerodynamic shapes.*

Fireworks *Often very hot and fluid lava is charged with gas when it first breaks the surface early in an eruption, and it comes shooting out like an exploding can of fizzy drink. Red-hot lava can spurt up to 200 metres (600 ft) in the air from a circular vent to produce a fire fountain.*

Eruption in progress

An erupting volcano is a dramatic and sometimes beautiful spectacle to watch from a safe distance, but it can also be dangerous and very destructive. This illustration shows many different types of eruptions and a variety of volcanic deposits, but we would never see a real volcano doing all of these things at once.

Pyroclastic flow *These superheated currents of hot gas and ash shoot rapidly down the side of a volcano during an eruption.*

Ash fall

After lying dormant for centuries the sleeping Soufrière Hills volcano on the Caribbean island of Montserrat came alive with a series of ash eruptions in 1995. The island's capital of Plymouth was abandoned in 1997 after it was buried by ash and pyroclastic flows.

Pahoehoe flow *The ancient Hawaiians gave us this word for lava that flows smoothly over the ground surface to produce a flat, or sometimes gently folded, surface that can look like coils of rope.*

Volcanic
Landscapes

Volcanoes have helped shape Earth's crust since the planet was born, producing dramatic mountains, craters and plateaus, as well as rolling hills, islands and fertile farmlands. It is easy to identify a volcano when it is erupting, or by its distinctive shape or deposits if it is dormant or recently extinct. But volcanism can leave its mark on the landscape even hundreds of millions of years after the eruptions have ceased. Often the clues are quite subtle and it takes the trained eye of a geologist to spot them.

Dormant volcano *Some volcanoes can lie quiet for many centuries between eruptions, allowing plants, animals and people to live on the rich land in the mountain's shadow. Yet volcanoes that awaken infrequently are some of the most dangerous.*

Volcanic island *Volcanoes that form beneath the sea can grow to create islands. If a volcano stops growing before it reaches the surface, it is called a seamount.*

Living with volcanoes *Volcanic soil is usually very rich and, in spite of the danger, the areas near volcanoes are often densely populated.*

Land made from fire
This is an imaginary landscape, but the volcanic features shown can be found all over the world. You can be thousands of kilometres away from the closest active volcano and still be surrounded by volcanic landforms.

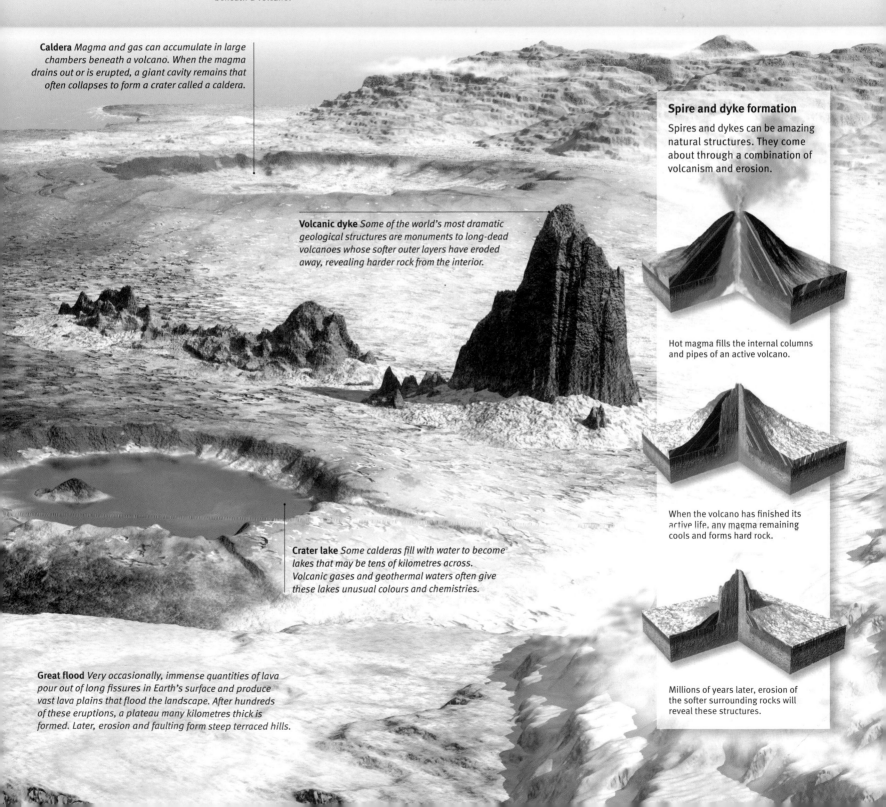

Caldera formation

Calderas often form as an intermediate stage between repeated eruptions and can often be recognised millions of years after the volcano is extinct.

Major eruptions can release huge volumes of magma from the chamber beneath a volcano.

Continued eruption can partially empty the chamber, leaving an empty space beneath the volcano.

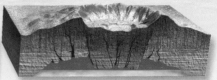

A large caldera is formed when the weight of the volcano collapses along ring faults and falls into the chamber.

Caldera *Magma and gas can accumulate in large chambers beneath a volcano. When the magma drains out or is erupted, a giant cavity remains that often collapses to form a crater called a caldera.*

Volcanic dyke *Some of the world's most dramatic geological structures are monuments to long-dead volcanoes whose softer outer layers have eroded away, revealing harder rock from the interior.*

Crater lake *Some calderas fill with water to become lakes that may be tens of kilometres across. Volcanic gases and geothermal waters often give these lakes unusual colours and chemistries.*

Great flood *Very occasionally, immense quantities of lava pour out of long fissures in Earth's surface and produce vast lava plains that flood the landscape. After hundreds of these eruptions, a plateau many kilometres thick is formed. Later, erosion and faulting form steep terraced hills.*

Spire and dyke formation

Spires and dykes can be amazing natural structures. They come about through a combination of volcanism and erosion.

Hot magma fills the internal columns and pipes of an active volcano.

When the volcano has finished its active life, any magma remaining cools and forms hard rock.

Millions of years later, erosion of the softer surrounding rocks will reveal these structures.

Thermal Springs and
Geysers

Almost everywhere on Earth, temperatures increase the deeper it is below the surface. This is especially so near volcanoes. When groundwater circulates through hot rock, it heats up, becomes less dense and then tries to force its way to the surface. Places where hydrothermal waters naturally vent on the surface are called thermal springs. Occasionally, subterranean chambers become filled and pressurised with hot water that periodically bursts forth on the surface in an explosion of water called a geyser. In some countries scientists and engineers use this hot water to heat homes and to make electricity. It is one of the cleanest ways of generating power because the main by-product is steam.

Simian spring

It is not only people who enjoy bathing in thermal springs. This troop of Japanese macaques are famous for escaping the winter cold in the thermal springs near the Shiga Kogen volcano in Japan.

Steam world

Hydrothermal areas can be found on land and beneath the sea, with water temperatures ranging from hot tap water to boiling water or even hotter steam. The waters can be rich with unusual chemical salts and often carry the rotten-egg smell of hydrogen sulphide gas.

Rock power *Geothermal power stations use hot thermal waters brought up from below to generate electricity or hot water for nearby towns.*

Waterworks *Cold water is injected down a well into a geothermal reservoir, where it is heated and returned to the power plant. Geothermal water is usually too salty to use directly in electricity generation, so huge coils of pipes are used to transfer the heat to fresh water to drive the turbines.*

Hot mud *Long-term continuous discharge of geothermal water can turn the surrounding rock into thick mud, forming gurgling "mud pots" or "mud cauldrons" at the thermal spring.*

Stages of a geyser

Geysers are a very rare phenomenon because at least three specific conditions must exist: plenty of groundwater; geothermal heat; and pressure- and watertight plumbing.

Groundwater heats up when it approaches hot rock and magma.

Cold water from above acts like a lid on the hot water below and pressure begins to build.

Eventually the pressure of the hot water exceeds that of the cold water and the system bursts forth as a boiling geyser.

Sculpted by water *Many geothermal areas feature terraces of carbonate, silicate or sulphide minerals deposited from the hot waters.*

What a rush *Geysers are periodic explosions of geothermal water from beneath the surface. Old Faithful in Yellowstone National Park (USA) and Geysir (southwestern Iceland) are two famous examples.*

Spring into it *Many thermal springs are popular vacation spots, especially where hot water mixes with cooler river or lake water to produce water of more comfortable temperature for bathing.*

Where the geyser sleeps *Below every geyser is a subterranean cavity that fills up with water and gases between each geyser eruption.*

Volcanologists
In the Field

Volcanologists are scientists who study volcanoes using methods from geology, chemistry, geography, mineralogy, physics and sociology to understand how volcanoes form, when and how often they might erupt and how eruptions affect people and the landscape. An important part of a volcanologist's work happens in the field, where many different measurements are made to learn about what a volcano is doing or did in the past. Other measurements are made in the laboratory or by the watchful eyes of satellites. It takes dedicated teams of scientists to gather and interpret all of this data, which is used to keep people informed about volcanic hazards.

Volcanologists at work

Volcanologists bring many special tools to the field for volcano study. Active volcanoes are dynamic and exciting workplaces, but volcanologists must prepare carefully for fieldwork and always be aware of the hazards.

Survey says *Careful surveys are made to detect the slightest changes in a volcano's topography. A bulge in the surface may indicate that an eruption is on the way.*

The easy way up *Helicopters help volcanologists reach remote volcanoes and cover lots of ground, but pilots need special skills to navigate the often rugged terrain and hot, particle-filled air.*

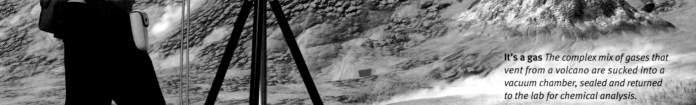

It's a gas *The complex mix of gases that vent from a volcano are sucked into a vacuum chamber, sealed and returned to the lab for chemical analysis.*

Electronic nose *Scientists use a correlation spectrometer to measure sulphur dioxide emitted from a volcano. Monitoring this dangerous gas helps scientists understand what is happening inside the volcano.*

Clues in the rock
Volcanologists often take rock samples to the laboratory to study their internal structure, mineralogy and composition. One way to do this is to view a thin slice of rock under a polarising light microscope, which reveals minerals in vivid colour.

Watch out! *Volcanologists never know when a small explosion might send hot rock fragments or gases their way, so they work in teams and keep a close watch on their surroundings.*

Hot work *You really feel the heat when you are up close and personal with a 1,200°C (2,200°F) lava flow. Specially designed thermal suits keep volcanologists cool when they sample molten lava.*

When the
Earth Moves

If you feel a shaking, bouncing or rocking motion of the ground, you are probably experiencing an earthquake. Earthquakes, and milder tremors, occur whenever rocks on either side of deep faults in Earth's crust suddenly break and slide past each other. The strength and duration of earthquakes depend on many factors, such as how deep in Earth the rupture was, how much stress the rocks were feeling before the fault slipped and the kinds of rocks involved. Many earthquakes occur because some rocks in the crust resist the movements deep within Earth that cause plates to separate, collide and slide past each other. Other quakes occur when huge weights build upon or are rapidly removed from the crust.

The Richter scale

American seismologist Charles Richter developed this earthquake magnitude scale in 1935. Each step on the scale represents a tenfold increase in earthquake power. That means that magnitude 7 is 10 times stronger than magnitude 6, and 100 times stronger than magnitude 5.

Broken earth

About 500,000 earthquakes are detected in the world each year. Most are too mild to be felt by people, but about 100 a year are strong enough to cause damage.

KINDS OF FAULTS

Faults are cracks in the crust where rock has moved at least once in the past. They are classified by the direction of their motion. Movement along faults is often a slow creep, but larger, sudden shifts produce earthquakes. The biggest quakes rupture the surface and deform the ground.

Epicentre This is the point on the surface directly above the hypocentre.

Normal fault Rocks on one side of the fault slump lower than on the other side.

Thrust or reverse fault The rocks on one side of the fault are thrust up above those on the other side.

Hypocentre The hypocentre is where energy in strained rocks is suddenly released as earthquake waves.

Transcurrent or strike-slip fault Rocks on either side of the fault slide past each other.

The modified Mercalli scale

Introduced in 1902 by Italian volcanologist Giuseppe Mercalli, the Mercalli scale measures earthquake intensity by the local effects on Earth's surface. As with the Richter scale, the modified Mercalli scale (so called because of its many updates) is often used to describe earthquakes to the public, but seismologists have now developed new measures of seismic energy.

I
Instrumental
Felt by very few people; barely noticeable

II
Feeble
Felt by a few people, especially on upper floors

III
Slight
Noticeable indoors, especially on upper floors; hanging objects swing

IV
Moderate
Felt by many indoors, few outdoors; dishes, windows and doors rattle

V
Rather strong
Felt by almost everyone, sleeping people wake; small objects moved; trees and poles may shake

VI

trong

t by everyone;
difficult to walk;
some heavy
furniture moved;
some plaster
alls; chimneys
ay be slightly
aged

VII

Very Strong

Difficult to stand;
slight to moderate
damage in well-built,
ordinary structures;
considerable damage
to poorly built
structures; some
chimneys broken

VIII

Destructive

Considerable
damage to ordinary
buildings; severe
damage to poorly
built structures;
heavy furniture
overturned; some
walls collapse

IX

Ruinous

Considerable
damage to specially
built structures;
buildings shifted off
foundations; ground
cracked noticeably;
underground pipes
crack

X

Disastrous

Most masonry and
frame structures and
their foundations
destroyed; ground
badly cracked;
landslides; railroad
tracks bend

XI

Very Disastrous

Few, if any, structures
standing; bridges
destroyed; wide
cracks in ground;
waves seen on
ground

XII

Catastrophic

Total destruction;
ground moves in
waves; heavy objects
thrown in the air

Earthquake
Preparation

Strong and gentle, extended and brief, tremors and quakes shake our Earth many times each day. We know how and why earthquakes and tremors occur, but not how to predict or prevent this awesome force of nature. But we can prepare for the inevitable. Studies of past earthquake frequency, type, size, ground rupture patterns and building damage allow seismologists and engineers to select less-hazardous sites for buildings and roads, and to design structures better able to withstand the swaying, rolling or pogo-stick motions of earthquakes. Being prepared also means having an efficient plan for responding to earthquake-related emergencies immediately after they happen.

AMURING PAGODAS

M any of Japan's Buddhist pagodas have stood for more than a thousand years, surviving countless earthquakes that have destroyed buildings around them. Modern engineers have only recently unravelled the ancient secrets of their design.

Jiggling joints
The flexible timber parts of a pagoda are slotted together without nails. During an earthquake they jostle about, dissipating the seismic energy.

Swingers The five storeys of a pagoda can swing independently of one another. During an earthquake the pagoda does a kind of "snake dance", keeping the building balanced.

Hard knocks
A massive central pillar dampens the vibration when the storeys move.

Top-heavy A tuned mass damper is a heavy weight installed at the top of a tall building. It is designed to move in the opposite direction of the building, keeping it steady when the wind blows or the ground shakes.

Braced for the worst Diagonal cross-bracing stops the building from moving more than it should.

Training for tremors
In some parts of the world, earthquake drills are a regular part of school life. Underneath a desk is a safe place to get to when an earthquake starts.

Shaken, not disturbed

Every year architects and engineers discover ways to build earthquake-resistant structures and to improve the safety of older ones. But these technologies are expensive, and tragically, earthquakes in less-developed regions of the world still regularly cause massive loss of life and property.

All together now *In many earthquake-prone cities engineers have put electricity, gas, water and telephone lines together in a single, specially strengthened tunnel.*

Pillar of strength *Concrete columns reinforced with spirals of steel are good at resisting the flexing and shaking forces of an earthquake.*

Slip and slide *A linear slider foundation allows the whole building to move horizontally, dissipating energy rather than breaking apart*

Bouncy building *This connection between the building and its foundation allows the building to bounce up and down during an earthquake.*

The Making of a
Tsunami

Tsunamis—the name is Japanese for "great harbour waves"—are caused by a jolt to the ocean floor from an earthquake, volcanic eruption or landslide. These giant waves may travel for thousands of kilometres but remain unnoticed as they pass under ships. A rise in the ocean floor near a coastline acts as a brake at the bottom of the wave. This forces the tsunami to slow down and rush upward, sometimes as towering walls of water called "wave trains" that crash onto land. The power of the waves batters and floods the coast, and can cause enormous damage and loss of life.

Tsunami disasters

1. **1946** Alaskan quake generates a tsunami. Hours later it kills 159 people in Hawaii.
2. **1964** Waves from an Alaskan quake kill 122 as they sweep down the West Coast.
3. **1896** A tsunami hits Los Angeles on the Californian coast.
4. **1960** A tsunami kills 1,000 in Chile and 61 in Hawaii.
5. **1775** An earthquake in Lisbon generates a tsunami. More than 60,000 die.
6. **1883** Krakatau erupts and a tsunami sweeps over Indonesia. 36,000 people die.
7. **2004** A powerful earthquake triggers waves that travel thousands of kilometres to crash onto the coastlines of at least 14 Asian and African countries. More than 225,000 people die.
8. **1976** A tsunami kills more than 5,000 people in the Philippines.
9. **1998** A tsunami strikes the north coast of Papua New Guinea, killing 2,000 people.
10. **1896** The Sanriku tsunami strikes Japan and kills more than 26,000 people.

Submarine earthquake

Most tsunamis form when an earthquake occurs deep in the ocean. Tectonic plates grind together, Earth's crust moves, water is disturbed and powerful shock waves form.

Spiralling forces *The powerful shock waves of energy spread out, rather like ripples when a stone is thrown into a pond. The waves can race across oceans for thousands of kilometres at speeds of up to 800 kilometres (500 mi) an hour—as fast as a jet plane.*

Before the tsunami
There is no sign of danger, but a tsunami can travel across an entire ocean in just one day. Early-warning systems are making it easier for scientists to predict when and where a tsunami will hit.

Water retreats
The peaceful bay is drained, as if someone had pulled a giant bath plug and let the water out. Bay water meets the developing tsunami just offshore.

Disaster strikes
The water rushes back to the beach. Walls of water, up to 30 metres (100 ft) high, crash on the shore and push inland with unstoppable force.

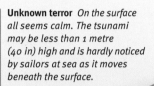

Unknown terror *On the surface all seems calm. The tsunami may be less than 1 metre (40 in) high and is hardly noticed by sailors at sea as it moves beneath the surface.*

At the shore *As the waves move closer to the shore, their speed decreases and their height increases. The tsunami arrives as a series of crests and troughs, between 10 and 45 minutes apart.*

Seismologists
In the Field

Seismologists are scientists who study earthquakes. They use information from geology, physics, civil engineering and geography to understand the reasons why earthquakes occur and the damage they cause. Seismologists also work with engineers to improve building codes and construction methods to make cities safer. Fieldwork is an important part of seismology. Many different measurements are made to learn about ground motion and deformation around earthquake faults, past and present. Other measurements are made in the laboratory to determine how materials behave when they encounter seismic waves.

Seismic waves

Energy generated by an earthquake travels in the form of waves through the surrounding rock. There are four kinds of seismic waves: two waves that travel through the interior of Earth, and two slower, more destructive waves that travel just under Earth's surface.

P-waves Primary, or pressure, waves pulse quickly through Earth's interior to the surface. These are the first waves felt in an earthquake.

GPS unit *A GPS (Global Positioning System) unit gives accurate readings of ground movement over time.*

ANIMAL INSTINCT

Many people, since at least the time of the ancient Greeks, have observed strange animal behaviour in the hours before an earthquake and have concluded that the animals could sense what was to come. It is unclear what they might be sensing and how. One theory is that animals can detect small changes in Earth's local magnetic field that are known to precede a quake. Unfortunately, scientific tests of earthquake occurrences and patterns of animal behaviour have not yet found a particular animal response that is reliable enough to predict earthquakes.

Magnetometer *A magnetometer detects the direction or intensity of Earth's magnetic field. Earthquakes are often preceded by small, ultralow-frequency variations in the local magnetic field.*

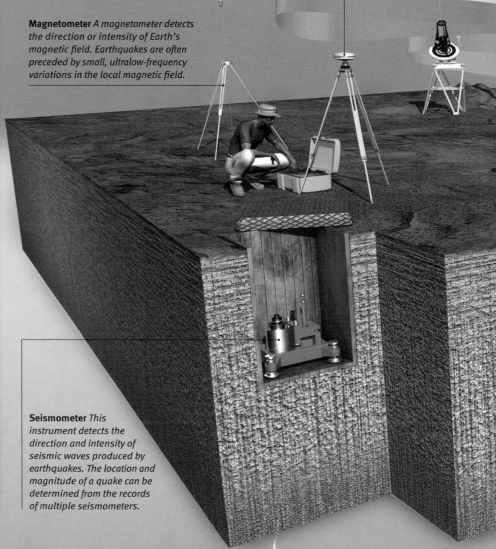

Seismometer *This instrument detects the direction and intensity of seismic waves produced by earthquakes. The location and magnitude of a quake can be determined from the records of multiple seismometers.*

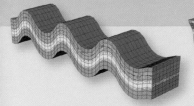

S-waves Secondary, or shear, waves shift material sideways as they propagate through Earth's interior at about half the speed of P-waves.

Love waves Love waves are side-to-side shearing motions of Earth's surface. They move more slowly than P- or S-waves.

Rayleigh waves Rayleigh waves cause the ground surface to deform like waves on the ocean. These are the slowest of the four seismic wave types.

Ancient seismometer

The ancient Chinese scientist and inventor Zhang Heng produced a device for detecting tremors in the year AD132. When disturbed, a pendulum within the bronze chamber caused a dragon's mouth to open and drop a ball into the mouth of a toad.

Satellite laser ranging *Seismologists aim laser beams at mirrors mounted on satellites to detect small movements before or after a quake.*

Seismic truck *These trucks create seismic waves by thumping the ground with a hydraulic piston. Equipment in a monitoring van records how the waves travel through the ground.*

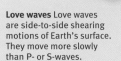

With a trace *Traditionally seismometers recorded earthquakes and tremors by drawing a line on a moving strip of paper. Today, nearly all seismometers record directly to computer memory.*

Borehole strain meter *These devices are placed in deep holes in the rock around earthquake faults. They measure the amount of stress on the rocks and how the rocks are deforming.*

Creepmeter *A creepmeter measures the slow movement or deformation of rock under stress below the surface.*

Seismologists at work

The seismologists' tool kit is full of specialised gear to study earthquake faults and ground motion. But they also need simple tools, such as a hammer to break up rocks, and a shovel to dig trenches into surface faults.

Locator map This map of the world shows you exactly where the featured event occurred. Look for the large red dot on each map.

THE SAN FRANCISCO EARTHQUAKE

DATE: **18 April 1906**

DURATION: **45–60 seconds**

RICHTER SCALE: **7.8–8.3**

MERCALLI SCALE: **VII–IX**

DEATH TOLL: **478 (official); 3,000–6,000 (estimated)**

Fast facts Fast facts at your fingertips give you essential information on each event being explored.

Side bar This side bar indicates how powerful the event was as measured by Volcanic Explosivity Index (volcanoes) or Richter scale (earthquakes).

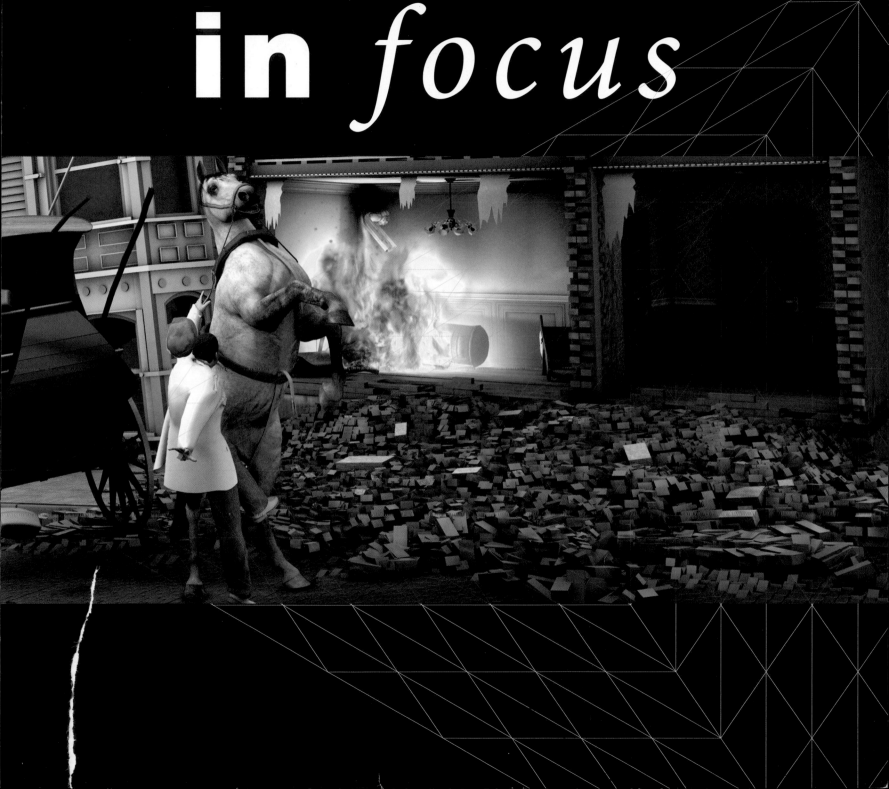

in *focus*

VEI 9
VEI 8
VEI 7
VEI 6
VEI 5
VEI 4
VEI 3
VEI 2
VEI 1

TOBA: THE FACTS

DATE: Approximately 73,500 years ago

VOLCANIC EXPLOSIVITY INDEX: 8

ERUPTION TYPE: Ultra-Plinian

ERUPTIVE VOLUME: Approximately 2,800 cubic kilometres (670 cu. mi)

DEATH TOLL: Unknown

Awesome ash cloud Ash spread far and wide during the Toba eruption, leaving deposits 9 metres (30 ft) thick in Malaysia and up to 15 centimetres (6 in) thick in far-off India and the Bay of Bengal.

Toba

Visit peaceful Lake Toba on the Indonesian island of Sumatra today, and you would never realise you were standing at the site of the largest volcanic eruption in human history. The lake is actually a caldera about 90 kilometres long by 30 kilometres across (55 x 20 mi). Scientists believe that around 73,500 years ago it unleashed a catastrophic eruption that spread volcanic ash and gases across the globe. The eruption probably lasted only a couple of weeks, but its effects were widely felt as a dramatic global cooling that lasted six years. This brought about changes to landscapes, forests and wildlife during a critical period of human development.

Longest winter

After the Toba eruption, our Stone Age ancestors must have suffered greatly from long, cold years of reduced food supply. Some scientists have speculated that this eruption brought humans to the brink of extinction.

Toba today The Lake Toba region is still volcanically active. Samosir Island, in the middle of the lake, is being pushed up out of the water by a swelling dome of magma beneath it. It is now the largest island within an island on Earth.

Toba
Eruptive volume
2,800 km³
(670 mi³)

La Garita
Eruptive volume
5,000 km³
(2,200 mi³)

Biggest bang The Toba eruption was the biggest that humans have ever lived through, but it is not the largest volcanic eruption we know of. The La Garita eruption in the western United States some 27 million years ago was almost twice as big.

Deadly haze
Volcanic ash and sulphur dioxide aerosols injected into the stratosphere formed a thin layer surrounding the globe, partially blocking the Sun's warming rays. This caused a long volcanic winter.

Altitude

km	mi
25	15
20	
15	10
10	5
5	
0	0

VEI 9

VEI 8

VEI 7

VEI 6

VEI 5

VEI 4

VEI 3

VEI 2

VEI 1

KRAKATAU: THE FACTS

DATE: 27 August 1883

VOLCANIC EXPLOSIVITY INDEX: 6

ERUPTION TYPE: Plinian/Ultra-Plinian

ERUPTIVE VOLUME: 20 cubic kilometres (5 cu. mi)

DEATH TOLL: 36,417

Ocean blast

An intense cloud of gas and ash shoots 80 kilometres (50 mi) up from Earth's surface during the final cataclysmic eruption at Krakatau. There were four huge explosions that occurred over a period of about four hours. The final explosion was the biggest of all.

Krakatau

Krakatau finally blew its top in August 1883 after three months of intensifying activity. The eruption made the loudest sound probably ever heard by humans and rates as the most powerful volcanic explosion ever witnessed. The eruption obliterated the volcanic cone of Krakatau and destroyed the island on which it sat. Many thousands of people were killed when tsunamis generated by hot pyroclastic flows entering the ocean enveloped the neighbouring parts of Indonesia. Ash from the eruption spread around the globe, causing unusually cool weather and glorious sunsets for many months. Today a new volcanic cone, Anak Krakatau, has risen from the seafloor where Krakatau once stood.

Krakatau scream
Volcanic particles high in the atmosphere produced vivid sunsets for months after the eruption. This famous painting by Norwegian Edvard Munch is thought to depict such a sunset seen in Oslo at the opposite side of Earth.

Blowing its t[...]
Video footage rev[...]
began, it took less[...]
of Mount St Hele[...]
cataclysmic explo[...]

A forest flatten[...]
Trees were scatt[...]
hundreds of squ[...]
were flattened b[...]
racing down the[...]

AFTER THE BLAST

Volcanologists are not sure why the Krakatau blast was so big, though it probably was due to an explosive reaction between magma and seawater.

Before and after
In the final stages of the eruption, most of Krakatau Island sank into the sea. The original area of the island is shown as pale green in the map above. Ash deposited in the eruption increased the size of the other islands that ringed the older Krakatau caldera.

Ash and noise pattern
The volcanic ash (grey) from the eruption spread mostly to the north-west. The sounds of the successive volcanic blasts (red) reverberated throughout the region and were heard up to 4,500 kilometres (2,800 mi) away.

VEI 9
VEI 8
VEI 7
VEI 6
VEI 5
VEI 4
VEI 3
VEI 2
VEI 1

10

VEI 9
VEI 8
VEI 7
VEI 6
VEI 5
VEI 4
VEI 3
VEI 2
VEI 1

9

8

7

6

5

RICHTER SCALE

LISBON: THE FACTS

DATE: **1 November 1755**

DURATION: **3.5–6 minutes**

RICHTER SCALE: **Estimated 8–9**

MERCALLI SCALE: **X (disastrous)**

DEATH TOLL: **60,000–100,000**

Mo

The United
world's bes
eruptions.
after lying
Scientists h
and althou
eruption, th
could only
eruption wa
top and sid
for kilometi
north-weste

❶ **March–**
magma
a consp
north fl
ground
for wee

Lisbon

Earth's crust ruptured 190 kilometres (120 mi) offshore from Lisbon, Portugal, on 1 November 1755, unleashing one of history's deadliest seismic disasters. Great buildings collapsed, large fissures opened up in city streets, a tsunami and then a fire raced through the city. Portugal's colonial ambitions were crippled. But with this terrible destruction came the beginnings of modern earthquake science. Rather than simply attributing the destruction to an act of God, Portugal's government instructed priests throughout the country to survey the damage and report on the population's experiences so that the nature of the earthquake could be better understood.

REBUILDING LISBON

Braced within
Timber bracing embedded within masonry walls helped prevent walls from collapsing.

Lisbon had to be almost completely rebuilt after the 1755 earthquake. For the first time in modern Europe, strict building rules were enforced to ensure that the new city could better withstand earthquake forces.

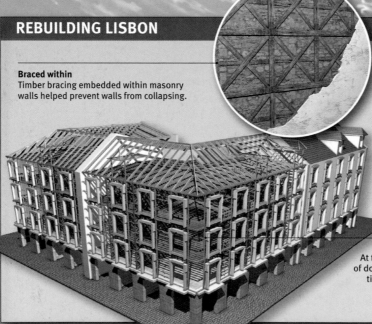

Cage frames
At the heart of the new buildings of downtown Lisbon were intricate timber frames that could safely dissipate seismic energy.

Wave of destruction
About half an hour after the quake, a massive tsunami crashed into Lisbon's harbour. Unfortunately, this is where many survivors had gathered, fearful that aftershocks would bring down more buildings in the city.

THE SAN FRANCISCO EARTHQUAKE

DATE: **18 April 1906**

DURATION: **45–60 seconds**

RICHTER SCALE: **7.8–8.3**

MERCALLI SCALE: **VII–IX**

DEATH TOLL: **478 (official); 3,000–6,000 (estimated)**

Disaster at dawn

San Franciscans awoke just after 5:00 a.m. 18 April 1906, to a violent shaking that was felt as far away as Los Angeles. Within a minute, the city was destroyed. Geologists had never seen such extensive ground rupturing or observed such differences in the severity of ground shaking, which was worst in areas with sediments and soils and much less severe in areas on bedrock. This gave them new understanding of earthquake hazards and how to use this knowledge for urban planning.

San Francisco

The city of San Francisco, California, sits astride the great San Andreas Fault, where the Pacific Plate grinds up against the North American Plate. The San Francisco region owes its rugged beauty to the geological forces of this continental margin. Deep below the city great frictional stresses build up within Earth's crust. Small earthquakes happen many times a year to relieve some of the stress, but occasionally a great earthquake occurs, as it did one morning in 1906, when perhaps as many as 6,000 people lost their lives.

Road chasm *All across the city giant cracks opened in the earth, resulting in broken gas lines and burst water pipes.*

SAN FRANCISCO ABLAZE

Most of the destruction of the 1906 earthquake resulted not from the earthquake itself but the subsequent fires that swept through the city, which burnt for four days and four nights.

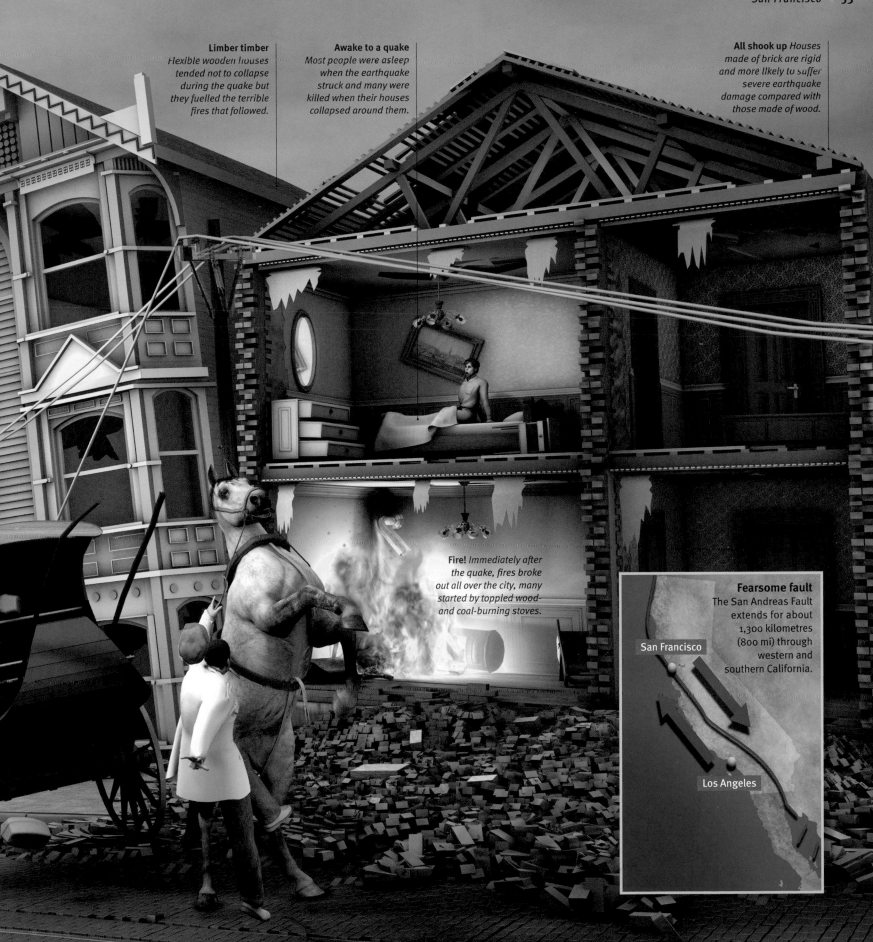

Limber timber
Flexible wooden houses tended not to collapse during the quake but they fuelled the terrible fires that followed.

Awake to a quake
Most people were asleep when the earthquake struck and many were killed when their houses collapsed around them.

All shook up *Houses made of brick are rigid and more likely to suffer severe earthquake damage compared with those made of wood.*

Fire! *Immediately after the quake, fires broke out all over the city, many started by toppled wood- and coal-burning stoves.*

Fearsome fault
The San Andreas Fault extends for about 1,300 kilometres (800 mi) through western and southern California.

San Francisco

Los Angeles

HEBGEN LAKE, MONTANA: THE FACTS

DATE: 17 August 1959

DURATION: 30–45 seconds

RICHTER SCALE: 7.5

MERCALLI SCALE: X (disastrous)

DEATH TOLL: 28

Stages of disaster

In just a few moments the landscape of the Madison River Canyon area was radically and permanently altered.

1 As the earthquake struck, the land north of Hebgen Lake moved upward in a sudden jolt, creating a fault scarp 6 metres (20 ft) high.

Hebgen Lake

Earthquakes have the power to permanently alter the landscape. One striking example is the Hebgen Lake earthquake that struck a remote corner of rural Montana, United States, in 1959. The ground ruptured more than 6 metres (20 ft) in places, and the quake produced a huge landslide that raced down the side of Madison Canyon, damming the Madison River and burying 28 campers. The waters of nearby Lake Hebgen were shaken like a rocking bathtub, and a wave crested its concrete dam four times. New hot springs and geysers sprung up in nearby Yellowstone National Park. Over the following month, accumulating water formed a new lake, called Earthquake Lake, behind the new earthen dam.

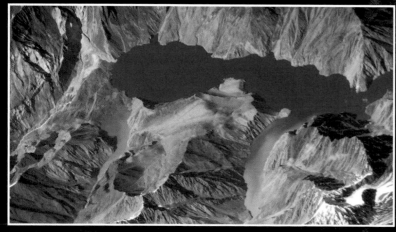

Lake Sarez, Tajikistan

In 1911 a powerful earthquake and landslide in Tajikistan, central Asia, created the largest dam in the world, man-made or natural. The resulting lake is 61 kilometres (38 mi) long and up to 500 metres (1,600 ft) deep. There are fears that another earthquake could break the dam and put millions of lives downstream in danger.

Mountain in motion

Because the earthquake struck in a remote area, the death toll was relatively low for such a powerful quake. However, 28 unfortunate vacationers lost their lives when the landslide overran the Rock Creek Campground.

2 A massive face of a mountain at the side of Madison Canyon broke free, sending an avalanche of rocks down to the river below. Meanwhile, waves generated by suddenly tilted ground beneath Hebgen Lake surged over the lake's concrete dam.

3 Landslide debris came to rest on the canyon floor, damming the Madison River and forming a new lake. Engineers later removed some of this material and formed a spillway to lower the lake and reduce the risk of the dam breaking.

KOBE, JAPAN: THE FACTS

DATE: 17 January 1995

DURATION: 20 seconds

RICHTER SCALE: 6.9–7.3

MERCALLI SCALE: X–XII (disastrous–catastrophic)

DEATH TOLL: 6,434

EURASIAN
PLATE

Kobe

Tokyo

PACIFIC
PLATE

PHILLIPINE
PLATE

Seismic map of Japan

The Kobe earthquake occurred when a strike-slip fault ruptured just north and west of the main seismic zone that skirts Japan's eastern coastline. Although virtually all of Japan is earthquake-prone, Kobe lies in a less active area and was considered relatively safe from major earthquakes. This map shows selected earthquakes recorded in Japan from 1961 to 1994. The bigger the circle, the more powerful the earthquake. Shallow earthquakes tend to be more powerful and destructive than ones which originate from deep within Earth.

Depth of hypocentre

- 0–50 km (0–31 mi)
- 50–100 km (31–62 mi)
- 100–150 km (62–93 mi)
- 150–200 km (93–124 mi)

Kobe

Early one morning in January 1995, residents of Kóbe, Japan, were startled awake when a fierce earthquake nearly levelled their city. The quake struck near Awaji Island, where the ground heaved up 3 metres (9 ft) during surface rupture of the fault. The seismic waves raced through the crust to Kobe, 20 kilometres (12 mi) away, causing one of the most costly natural disasters ever. The damage was extensive because the epicentre was so close to a large and densely populated city. Even worse, Kobe had been considered at low risk for severe earthquakes, and building codes were not as strict as in other parts of Japan.

Namazu and Kashima Traditionally, the Japanese blamed earthquakes on Namazu, a subterranean catfish. Usually the deity Kashima held Namazu down, but if Kashima's attention wandered, Namazu thrashed about, shaking the ground.

① Intact column In the reinforced columns, steel and concrete work together. Concrete supports the huge weight of the expressway while steel rods hold the concrete together and keep the forces vertical all along the length of the column.

② Earthquake The columns are not nearly so strong when horizontal forces are applied. During the earthquake small cracks begin to open and the bond between the steel and concrete is weakened.

Expressway collapse

The elevated Hanshin Expressway was hard hit by the earthquake, with damage to half of its concrete piers. Ten separate spans collapsed completely.

City in ruins

Factories, offices, schools and countless homes were all damaged beyond repair. More than six thousand Kobe residents were killed and another three hundred thousand people, one-third of the city's population, were left homeless.

3 Failure point As more concrete crumbles, only the steel rods support the expressway. They quickly buckle and twist, and the whole structure collapses.

10

9

8

7

6

5

INDIAN OCEAN TSUNAMI: THE FACTS

DATE: 26 December 2004

DURATION: 10 minutes

RICHTER SCALE: 9.3

MERCALLI SCALE: XI (very disastrous)

DEATH TOLL: Approximately 230,000

Earth shaker

This was a disaster of global proportions. Lives were lost on the shores of 13 nations, and citizens from a total of 55 nations were killed. The disaster took hours to unfold. The lines and numbers on the globe indicate how far the tsunami travelled each hour after the earthquake.

Indian Ocean

Tsunami

The whole Earth vibrated like a bell when the second largest earthquake ever recorded struck on 26 December 2004. The enormous, undersea Sumatra–Andaman earthquake lasted 10 minutes—the longest on record—and ruptured nearly 1,600 kilometres (1,000 mi) of seabed. The quake unleashed a series of tsunamis that devastated coastlines all around the Indian Ocean and killed hundreds of thousands of people in South-East Asia. Sadly, many would have survived had a multinational tsunami early-warning system been in place. Such a system is only now being established in the Indian Ocean.

Kerala, India *Tsunami waves can diffract around a land mass and change direction. Hundreds of people died on the "sheltered" west coast of India.*

Sea to sky The data is relayed to satellite.

Sky to ground The satellite transmits data to ground stations.

Tsunami early-warning systems

With the right technology in place, advanced warning of a tsunami's approach can be relayed from the open ocean back to shore. Communities at risk can then be alerted via sirens, radio and television broadcasts and cell phone messages.

Seafloor up The data is transmitted to a buoy on the surface.

Tsunameter At the heart of the system is a pressure sensor on the seabed. It can detect tsunami waves as small as 1 centimetre (0.4 in).

c. 6,000 metres (20,000 ft)

Port Elizabeth, South Africa *The most distant death attributed to the tsunami was a drowning in Port Elizabeth, about 8,000 kilometres (5,000 mi) from the epicentre.*

3

4

5

6

7

8

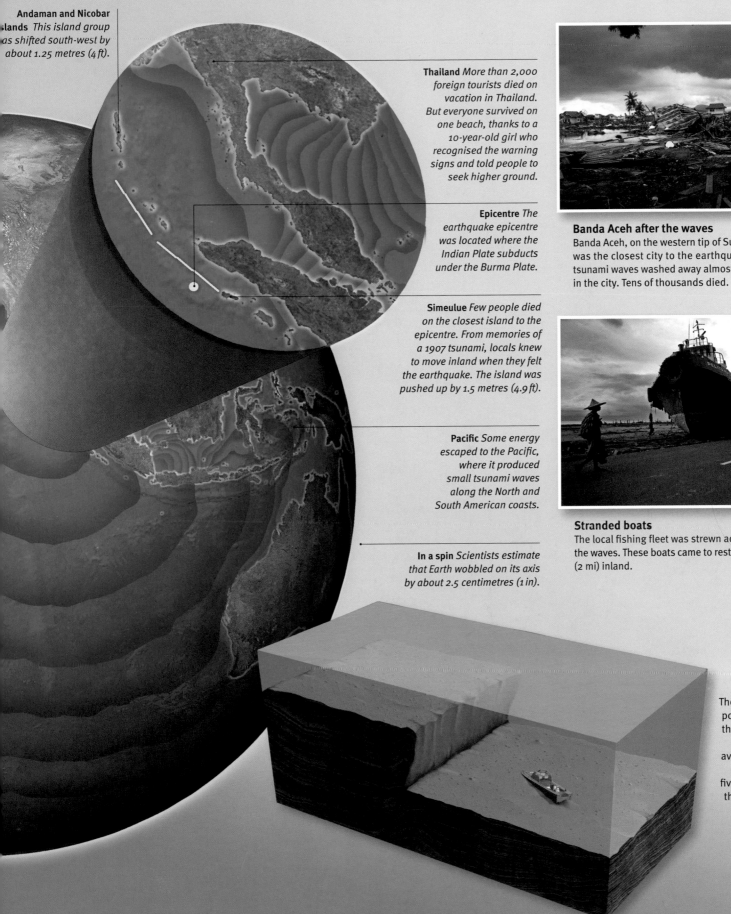

Andaman and Nicobar Islands *This island group has shifted south-west by about 1.25 metres (4 ft).*

Thailand *More than 2,000 foreign tourists died on vacation in Thailand. But everyone survived on one beach, thanks to a 10-year-old girl who recognised the warning signs and told people to seek higher ground.*

Epicentre *The earthquake epicentre was located where the Indian Plate subducts under the Burma Plate.*

Simeulue *Few people died on the closest island to the epicentre. From memories of a 1907 tsunami, locals knew to move inland when they felt the earthquake. The island was pushed up by 1.5 metres (4.9 ft).*

Pacific *Some energy escaped to the Pacific, where it produced small tsunami waves along the North and South American coasts.*

In a spin *Scientists estimate that Earth wobbled on its axis by about 2.5 centimetres (1 in).*

Banda Aceh after the waves

Banda Aceh, on the western tip of Sumatra in Indonesia, was the closest city to the earthquake epicentre. The tsunami waves washed away almost all of the buildings in the city. Tens of thousands died.

Stranded boats

The local fishing fleet was strewn across the landscape by the waves. These boats came to rest about three kilometres (2 mi) inland.

Seabed uplift

The tsunami waves were powered by a rupture in the seabed hundreds of kilometres long. On average, one side of the rupture came to rest five metres (16 ft) higher than the other. In some places the difference was as much as 20 metres (65 ft).

Worlds Alive

VOLCANOES AROUND THE WORLD

Volcano map
There are about 1,500
active volcanoes around
the world and many
more that are dormant
or extinct. This map
shows some notable
examples.

Legend

🔺 = Active volcano

🔼 = Dormant volcano

🔺 = Extinct volcano

▲ = Height

✳ = Last eruption

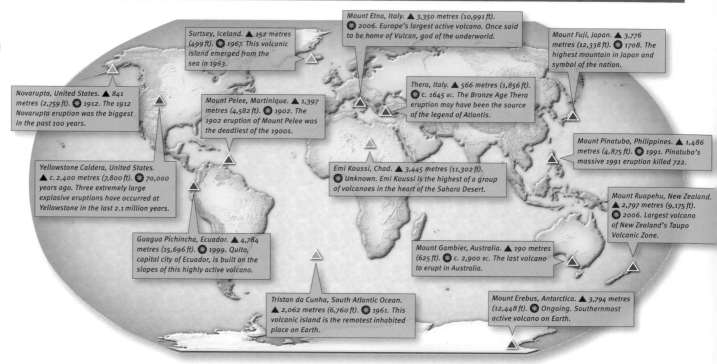

Surtsey, Iceland. ▲ 152 metres (499 ft). ✳ 1967. This volcanic island emerged from the sea in 1963.

Mount Etna, Italy. ▲ 3,350 metres (10,991 ft). ✳ 2006. Europe's largest active volcano. Once said to be home of Vulcan, god of the underworld.

Mount Fuji, Japan. ▲ 3,776 metres (12,338 ft). ✳ 1708. The highest mountain in Japan and symbol of the nation.

Novarupta, United States. ▲ 841 metres (2,759 ft). ✳ 1912. The 1912 Novarupta eruption was the biggest in the past 100 years.

Mount Pelee, Martinique. ▲ 1,397 metres (4,582 ft). ✳ 1902. The 1902 eruption of Mount Pelee was the deadliest of the 1900s.

Thera, Italy. ▲ 566 metres (1,856 ft). ✳ c. 1645 BC. The Bronze Age Thera eruption may have been the source of the legend of Atlantis.

Mount Pinatubo, Philippines. ▲ 1,486 metres (4,875 ft). ✳ 1991. Pinatubo's massive 1991 eruption killed 722.

Yellowstone Caldera, United States. ▲ c. 2,400 metres (7,800 ft). ✳ 70,000 years ago. Three extremely large explosive eruptions have occurred at Yellowstone in the last 2.1 million years.

Emi Koussi, Chad. ▲ 3,445 metres (11,302 ft). ✳ Unknown. Emi Koussi is the highest of a group of volcanoes in the heart of the Sahara Desert.

Mount Ruapehu, New Zealand. ▲ 2,797 metres (9,175 ft). ✳ 2006. Largest volcano of New Zealand's Taupo Volcanic Zone.

Guagua Pichincha, Ecuador. ▲ 4,784 metres (15,696 ft). ✳ 1999. Quito, capital city of Ecuador, is built on the slopes of this highly active volcano.

Mount Gambier, Australia. ▲ 190 metres (625 ft). ✳ c. 2,900 BC. The last volcano to erupt in Australia.

Tristan da Cunha, South Atlantic Ocean. ▲ 2,062 metres (6,760 ft). ✳ 1961. This volcanic island is the remotest inhabited place on Earth.

Mount Erebus, Antarctica. ▲ 3,794 metres (12,448 ft). ✳ Ongoing. Southernmost active volcano on Earth.

EARTHQUAKE RISK

Earthquake map
The chances of being
shaken up by an
earthquake depend on
where on Earth you are.
In many places you could
live a whole lifetime and
never feel the ground
move. In other places,
tremors are a regular
occurrence and the
risk of a destructive
earthquake is always
present.

Earthquake risk

⬜ = Low

🟫 = Medium

⬛ = High

⬛ = Very high

EARTHQUAKE THEORIES

Changing ideas

As long as people have felt the ground shake, they have sought to explain the frightening phenomenon of earthquakes. But it is only very recently that we have truly worked out what is happening beneath our feet.

A Hindu cosmos.

Religious and mythical explanations

For centuries, explanations for earthquakes were linked with religion and myth. For instance, according to an ancient Hindu myth, Earth is carried on the back of an elephant, which stands on a turtle that is balanced on a cobra. Whenever one moves, Earth trembles and shakes.

Ancient Greeks

The ancient Greek philosophers are the first people we know of to seek natural explanations for earthquakes. They speculated that within Earth there are vast caverns where wild winds blow. Earth shakes when the winds blow on the cavern roofs or break through to the surface.

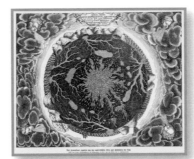

A cross section of Earth's interior from 1665.

Early modern Europe

The Italian artist and inventor Leonardo da Vinci theorised that Earth was composed of solid matter interspersed with water. If the balance between them is upset, sudden movements occur. In the 1660s the French philosopher René Descartes suggested that Earth was once as hot as the Sun and that it is still cooling and shrinking. These contractions created the mountains and cause earthquakes.

Modern times

Plate tectonic theory had its beginnings in 1915, when German scientist Alfred Wegener suggested that all the continents were once joined together and had subsequently drifted apart. This would explain why the outlines of the continents so often seem to fit together like a puzzle. Wegener could not explain how the continents moved, but research in the 1950s and 60s revealed the existence of tectonic plates and seafloor spreading. Plate tectonic theory has proved to be a convincing explanation for earthquakes and other geological phenomena.

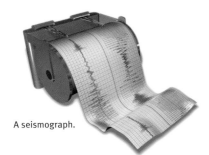

A seismograph.

VOLCANOES OUT OF THIS WORLD

Space shaper

Volcanoes are not restricted to Earth. In fact, judging by our own Solar System, volcanism seems to be quite a common phenomenon in the universe. Volcanoes have played a part in shaping the surface of all four inner rocky planets (Mercury, Venus, Earth and Mars) as well as some of the moons of the outer gas giants.

The Moon

Billions of years ago Earth's moon was volcanically active. The dark patches we can see on the surface are solidified lakes of molten lava.

Venus

Venus has many thousands of volcanoes. They are responsible for the planet's thick atmosphere. Scientists are not sure if any volcanoes are still active.

Mars

Mars is about half the size of Earth, but it boasts volcanoes that dwarf the tallest mountains on our planet. However, Mars is almost certainly volcanically extinct.

Io

Jupiter's moon Io is the most volcanically active body in the Solar System. It spews a noxious mixture of molten and gaseous sulphur dioxide from its surface.

Triton

Volcanoes are not always hot. In 1989 a passing space probe discovered huge geysers on Neptune's moon Triton that erupt with supercold liquid nitrogen.

INDIAN OCEAN TSUNAMI

Dead or missing by nationality

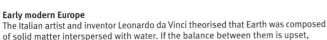

	1–10	11–100	101–1,000	1,001–10,000	10,001–100,000	100,001–200,000
* Indonesia: 167,540						
* Sri Lanka: 35,322						
* India: 16,269						
* Thailand: 5,996						
Germany: 552						
Sweden: 543						
* Somalia: 289						
Finland: 178						
United Kingdom: 149						
Switzerland: 111						
* Maldives: 108						
France: 95						
Norway: 84						
* Malaysia: 75						
Austria: 74						
* Myanmar: 61						
Japan: 44						
Italy: 40						
Hong Kong: 40						
Netherlands: 36						
United States: 31						
Australia: 26						
* South Africa: 23						
South Korea: 20						
Canada: 20						
* Tanzania: 13						
Belgium: 11						
China: 10						
* Seychelles: 2						
* Bangladesh: 2						
* Kenya: 1						

* = countries directly affected by the tsunami. (Note that 21 of the South African dead were killed in Thailand.)

Geysers around Neptune

This illustration shows Triton's geysers erupting with plumes of liquid nitrogen. This material rises about eight kilometres (5 mi) above the surface before raining down as nitrogen frost.

Glossary

a'a A type of lava flow that has a jagged surface when it cools and solidifies.

active volcano A volcano that produces eruptions of gas and lava. The bursts may be separated by weeks or many centuries.

aerosol Small particles and liquid droplets formed as volcanic gases cool in the air.

aftershock A tremor that follows a large earthquake and originates at or near the hypocentre of the initial quake.

ash Fine pieces of rock and lava ejected during volcanic eruptions.

asthenosphere A layer in Earth's upper mantle so soft that it can flow.

black smoker A vent situated on an ocean ridge, which emits hot, mineral-laden water.

caldera A large, circular depression formed when a volcano collapses above its magma chamber.

cinder Small fragments of volcanic rock, usually full of trapped gas bubbles, ejected during a volcanic eruption. Also called scoria.

conduit A wide pipe inside a volcano through which magma moves from the interior to a vent.

continent One of Earth's seven main land masses: Africa, Antarctica, Asia, Australia, Europe, North America and South America. The land masses include edges beneath the ocean as well as dry land.

continental margin The edges of continental land masses consisting of the coastal zone and shallowly submerged lands near the coast.

convection current A current that transfers heat by moving material around, such as the movement of hot rock in the mantle.

convergent margin A boundary between two tectonic plates that are moving towards each other.

core Earth's centre. It consists of a solid inner core and a molten outer core, both of which are made of an iron-nickel alloy.

crater A circular depression formed as a result of a volcanic eruption (volcanic crater) or by the impact of a meteorite (impact crater).

crater lake A water-filled crater. It may be filled on a seasonal or permanent basis.

crust The outermost solid layer of Earth, which varies from a thickness of 5 kilometres (3 mi), under the youngest seafloor, to 72 kilometres (45 mi), under the thickest parts of continents.

divergent margin A boundary between two tectonic plates that are moving apart.

dormant volcano A volcano that is not currently active but that could erupt again.

dyke A sheet of igneous rock formed when magma rises through a crack.

epicentre The point on Earth's surface that is directly above the hypocentre, or starting point, of an earthquake.

eruption The volcanic release of lava, ash or gas from Earth's interior onto the surface and into the atmosphere.

extinct volcano A volcano that has shown no sign of activity for a long period and is considered unlikely to erupt again.

fault margin A crack in rock layers created by the rocks shifting in opposite directions or at different speeds.

fissure A fracture or crack in the ground. In volcanic areas, a fissure may be associated with a line of vents (known as fissure volcanoes).

flood basalt A flow of basalt lava that spreads over a large area. Many layers of these flows form a basalt plateau.

fumarole A vent that emits hot volcanic gases or steam.

geologist A scientist who studies the physical and chemical processes that have shaped Earth's surface and interior today or in the past.

geothermal energy Energy that can be extracted from Earth's interior heat, whether from hot rocks, hot water or steam.

geyser A surface vent that periodically spouts a fountain of boiling water.

hot spot A persistent and nearly stationary zone of melting within Earth's mantle.

hydrothermal activity Any process involving the formation or movement of water and dissolved chemicals by interaction with hot rock.

hypocentre The place within Earth where energy in strained rocks is suddenly released as earthquake waves.

igneous Rock formed when magma cools and solidifies.

island arc An arc-shaped chain of volcanic islands that forms above subducting seafloor.

laccolith A body of igneous rock formed when rising magma cools before erupting at the surface. Laccoliths often push overlying rock layers upward.

lahar A flow of hot mud created by a volcanic eruption.

lateral fault A fault along which rocks have moved sideways. It is sometimes called a strike-slip or transform fault.

lava Molten rock that has erupted from a volcano onto Earth's surface.

lava bomb A large lump of molten lava or hot rock thrown from a volcano that attains a nearly spherical shape as it cools in flight. A lava bomb is usually more than 32 millimetres (1.25 in) across.

lava dome A mound of thick, sticky lava that grows directly over a vent at the top of, or on the flanks of, a volcano.

lava tube An underground river of lava formed when the surface of an open lava channel solidifies.

liquefaction The change of sediment or soil into a fluid mass as a result of an earthquake.

lithosphere The rigid outer part of Earth, consisting of the crust and the uppermost part of the mantle.

magma Melted rock found inside Earth. It may solidify inside Earth or erupt at the surface to form lava.

magma chamber A pool of magma in the lithosphere from which volcanic materials may erupt.

magnitude The strength of an earthquake, based on the amount of energy released. Seismologists measure magnitude using the modified Richter Scale, which begins at zero and has no maximum.

mantle The thick layer between Earth's crust and the outer core. It includes the lower mantle and asthenosphere—the parts of the mantle that flow—and the lower lithosphere, which is the rigid uppermost part of the mantle.

mid-ocean ridge A long, raised ridge formed by volcanic action at the edges of diverging oceanic plates.

mineral A naturally formed solid with an ordered arrangement of atoms, found in Earth's crust.

mudflow A river of ash, mud and water set off by a volcanic eruption or earthquake. Mudflows triggered by volcanoes are also known as lahars.

normal fault A fracture in rock layers, where the upper side has moved downward relative to the other side along a plane inclined between 45 and 90 degrees.

pahoehoe A type of lava flow with a smooth, ropelike surface.

pillow lava Lava that forms rounded mounds by cooling quickly after erupting underwater or flowing into water.

plug A column of volcanic rock formed when lava solidifies inside the vent of a volcano.

plume A rising column of hot rock in the mantle, within which melting can take place. The term can also apply to a large column of ash above a volcano.

primary wave A seismic wave, also known as a P-wave, that compresses and expands rocks as it travels through them. It is called a primary wave because it is the wave that arrives first during an earthquake, before the secondary wave.

pumice A light-coloured, low-density, glassy volcanic rock that contains many cavities. It is so light that it can float in water.

pyroclastic flow A dense, heated mixture of volcanic gas, ash and rock fragments that travels at great speed down volcanic slopes. It forms as a result of the collapse of an eruption column or a lava dome.

reverse fault A fracture in rock layers, where the top side has moved upward relative to the other side along a plane inclined between 45 and 90 degrees.

rift valley A wide valley that forms when rock layers move apart and a central section drops downward as a result of normal faulting.

secondary wave A seismic wave, also known as an S-wave, that moves rocks from side to side as it passes through them. It is called a secondary wave because it is the second type of wave to arrive during an earthquake.

seismic Related to an earthquake or tremor.

seismologist A scientist who studies seismic waves produced by earthquakes to understand where and how they form or to study Earth's internal and surface structure.

seismology The study of Earth tremors, whether natural or artificially produced.

seismometer An instrument that detects, magnifies and records Earth's vibrations.

shield volcano A volcano that is much wider than it is tall, formed by repeated flows of lava. This type of volcano looks like a shield when viewed from above.

subduction The process in which one tectonic plate descends below another.

subterranean Related to things that are found or that occur underground.

surface wave A seismic wave that travels along Earth's surface. It arrives after primary and secondary waves and moves up and down or from side to side.

tectonic plate Rigid pieces of Earth's lithosphere that move over the asthenosphere.

tephra Particles or fragments ejected from a volcano of any size or shape.

thrust fault A fracture in rock layers, where the upper side rides over the top of the lower side at an angle of less than 45 degrees.

transform fault A fault along which rocks move in opposite directions or at different speeds. They are common at some plate margins.

tsunami A Japanese word for a sea wave produced by an earthquake, landslide or volcanic blast. It reaches its greatest height in shallow waters before crashing onto land.

vent An opening on the surface of a volcano through which lava and gas erupt.

volcano A typically circular landform from which molten rock and gases erupt.

volcanologist A scientist who studies eruptions and interior processes at active and inactive volcanoes.

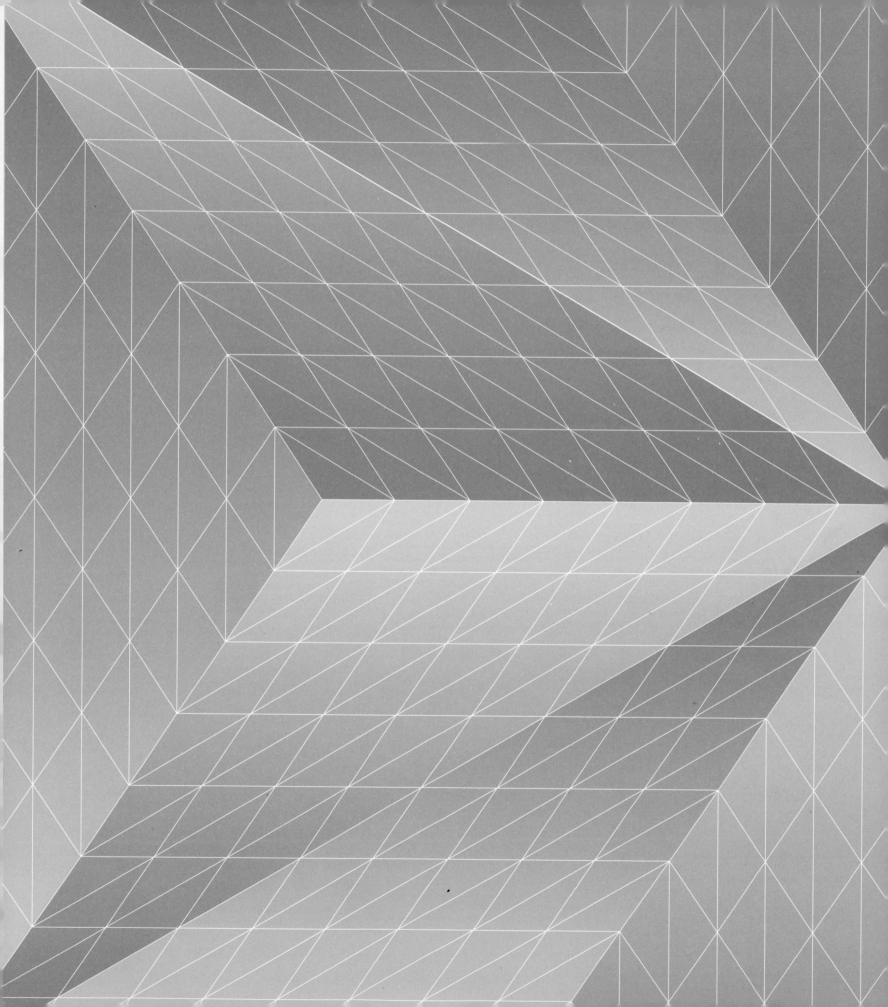